Contemporary Studies in Literature

Eugene Ehrlich, *Columbia University*
Daniel Murphy, *City University of New York*
Series Editors

Volumes include:

WILLIAM FAULKNER, edited by
Dean M. Schmitter

F. SCOTT FITZGERALD, edited by
Kenneth E. Eble

ERNEST HEMINGWAY, edited by
Arthur Waldhorn

D. H. LAWRENCE, edited by Leo Hamalian

WALT WHITMAN, edited by Arthur Golden

W. B. YEATS, edited by Patrick J. Keane

Ernest
Hemingway

a collection of criticism edited by Arthur Waldhorn

McGraw-Hill Book Company

New York • St. Louis • San Francisco • London • Düsseldorf
Kuala Lumpur • Mexico • Montreal • Panama • São Paulo
Sydney • Toronto • Johannesburg • New Delhi • Singapore

Grateful acknowledgment is made to the following for their permission to reprint from the works indicated: F. I. Carpenter, "Hemingway Achieves the Fifth Dimension," from *American Literature and the Dream,* copyright 1954. Reprinted by permission of Philosophical Library. Robert Evans, "Hemingway and the Pale Cast of Thought," *American Literature.* Reprinted by permission of the publisher; copyright 1966, Duke University Press, Durham, North Carolina. Daniel Fuchs, "Ernest Hemingway, Literary Critic," *American Literature.* Reprinted by permission of the publisher; copyright 1965, Duke University Press, Durham, North Carolina. John Graham, "Ernest Hemingway: The Meaning of Style," *Modern Fiction Studies,* copyright 1961, by Purdue Research Foundation, Lafayette, Indiana. E. M. Halliday, "Hemingway's Ambiguity: Symbolism and Irony," *American Literature.* Reprinted by permission of the publisher; copyright 1956, Duke University Press, Durham, North Carolina. Bern Oldsey, "The Snows of Ernest Hemingway," *Wisconsin Studies in Contemporary Literature,* 4 (Spring–Summer 1963), © 1963 by the Regents of the University of Wisconsin, pp. 172–198. Arthur Waldhorn, Chapter 1, "Life," from *A Reader's Guide to Ernest Hemingway* by Arthur Waldhorn. Copyright © 1972 by Arthur Waldhorn, reprinted by permission of Farrar, Straus, and Giroux, Inc. Philip Young, "The World and an American Myth," from *Ernest Hemingway: A Reconsideration* by Philip Young. Copyright © 1966 by Philip Young, reprinted by permission of the Pennsylvania State University Press.

123456789MUMU79876543

Library of Congress Cataloging in Publication Data

Waldhorn, Arthur, 1918–
Ernest Hemingway.

(Contemporary studies in literature)
Bibliography: p.
1. Hemingway, Ernest, 1899–1961.
PS3515.E37Z918   813'.5'2   73-160
ISBN 0-07-067800-6

to Put

Preface

What is there left to say about Hemingway? Is there another American writer in this century (with the possible exception of Norman Mailer) about whom everyone speaks or has spoken with such assurance or with so absolute a sense of personal possession? Many of the older generation of academic anglers, in fact, have spun their yarns and abandoned the old fishing site. Some left a heritage of wisecracks about Hemingway as a "frontiersman of the loins," or a Stein-stutterer who composed crises in cablese about a hero who is "a dull-witted, bovine, monosyllabic simpleton" and whose morality holds only "for wartime, for sport, for drinking, and for expatriates." Some, however, discovered more than material for raillery. Cyril Connolly discerned greatness in Hemingway because "he alone of living writers has saturated his books with the memory of physical pleasure, with sunshine and salt water, with food, wine and making love, and with the remorse which is the shadow of that sun." And Saul Bellow wrote of him as "the poet of the crippled state."

Today, a new breed of angler seems to be drifting back to the old stream, several of them determined to venture into the "bad" place—the sunless swamp of inner turbulence where Hemingway's Nick Adams feared to go lest the fishing prove "tragic." Often these compleat anglers rely upon archetypal myths or Freudian and Jungian depth charges to explode the secrets of Hemingway's art from the mottled deep of his psyche. Frequently, we learn more about the critic than about his quarry: Hemingway remains a slippery prey. The relationship between his life and his art has not been wholly explained despite the appearance of Carlos Baker's "authorized" biography. More important, Hemingway's esthetic and thematic worth needs—as a new generation revalues its inherited literary gods—to be assessed anew.

The essays collected here represent the points of view of older and younger critics alike, though never, it is hoped, in their extreme, more absurd attitudes. Each of these essays takes an overview rather than fixes upon a single work (though a single novel often receives detailed attention). My opening summary of Hemingway's career suggests rather than defines certain patterns interwoven in his life and art. All of the other studies have been selected to afford a range of critical attitudes and insights centered upon issues of style and theme. John Graham writes broadly about Hemingway's style, but his analysis of how Hemingway achieves immediacy and vitality through cumulative effects makes this study a necessary introduction to the essays that follow. E. M. Halliday's pioneer treatment of Hemingway's use of irony and symbolism opened a trail that Bern Oldsey follows but with a sensitive acumen of his own. The reader who observes their cautious markings will be less likely to fall into foolish traps set by symbol and allegory hunters. F. I. Carpenter's analysis of Hemingway's time sense is justly respected, whether or not one at last admires Hemingway's use of the eternal "now."

Daniel Fuchs locates Hemingway's fiction in the tradition of the novel of burlesque. As a result of his interest and skill in that tradition (his models include Cervantes, Fielding, and Anatole France), Hemingway was able, Fuchs argues, to fuse both style and subject matter as a means of ridiculing conventional modes of language and morality. But if Fuchs finds "a kind of resilience to his intelligence that is not often associated with it," Robert Evans retorts in his essay that Hemingway's cast of thought is at best pale. Hemingway's world, Evans insists, is "repetitious . . . and, finally . . . drearily predictable . . . not quite mansized." Philip Young does not agree. Indeed, he sees Hemingway's world as an integral myth—the Fall of Man—in the continuity of American experience.

The purpose of this collection is not to prove that Hemingway is either a marlin or a minnow. Rather is it intended to project thoughtful and divergently oriented analyses (with additional readings suggested in the appended bibliography) of the work of a major American writer of our century. Sources of the material used are listed in the acknowledgments on the copyright page of this volume. At best, this collection may stimulate further study by generations of young readers who must at last decide whether Hemingway deserves continuing respect and attention as a substantial creative force in American letters.

A. W.

The City College of The City University of New York, March 1972

Contents

Arthur Waldhorn

Artist and Adventurer: A Biographical Sketch

"Madame, it is always a mistake to know an author," Ernest Hemingway warns the Old Lady in *Death in the Afternoon* [144*]. About his preference for working in the morning or writing with a number 2 pencil, or his tastes in food, drink, guns, music, and art, Hemingway was never reticent. But when the questions touched feeling and motive, his responses were always elusive or coldly negative: "Let's give my life a miss." He wanted no biography written during his lifetime and hoped that none would be written until a century after his death. Only three years before he died, he wrote a codicil to his will insisting that none of his many letters ever be published. Nevertheless, Hemingway drew more attention to himself as a *man* and has had more non-literary copy written about him than any other American writer in the twentieth century.

One simple but compelling reason was his life style, as dramatic as his prose but far more baroque. For more than thirty of his forty years as a famous writer, his other "careers" as hunter, fisherman, skier, boxer, reporter, soldier, bull-ring and saloon *aficionado* were enthusiastically recorded by gossip columnists and mass-circulation magazines. In each decade his life style altered in details, but the essential pattern prevailed: Hemingway took the risks young men dream of taking and older men nostalgically wish they had taken. A youth from a safely bourgeois home in the Midwest, schooled to follow in that tradition, he opted for a wholly different and more perilous way.

The penalties for taking risks run high and Hemingway paid them. In war and peace, he was racked by disease and suffered

*Numbers in brackets refer to pages in the editions of Hemingway's works listed under "Primary Sources" in the Bibliography at the end of this volume.

1

hundreds of wounds—skull fracture, concussions, internal injuries. But, as he said, "My luck, she is running very good." He survived them all, all except the last, self-inflicted wound. There were other rewards too. People, for example. He formed extraordinary friendships (but carried on endless feuds with many friends).[1] He mingled intimately with Gary Cooper and Marlene Dietrich but as well with hunting guides in Africa, bullfighters in Spain, bartenders in Paris, and fishermen in Havana. To countless G.I.'s in France and Germany, he was self-identified as "Ernie Hemorrhoid, the poor man's Pyle." Moreover, he had four wives and a lot of money, more than a million dollars when he died.

So narrow a view of Hemingway the man tells little of the entire story, but it serves to place him at the outset where, as a man, he belongs—in the romantic tradition. Like Wordsworth, he preferred the common people; like Keats, he loved the sensuous and seemed "half in love with easeful death"; and like Byron most of all, he affected the heroic posture, Promethean rebel against the conventions of society. But such parallels are also too facile. Hemingway lived as an American in the twentieth century and his life (as well as his work) sounds the familiar notes of his violent time and his restless people: loneliness, alienation, and disillusion. Somehow, Hemingway's experience promised a triumph of the soul despite terror, seemed to assure that heroism was still possible, and that the artist knew the way.

One hears in all this the not-too-distant brassy ring of glamour and success. But there is a deeper resonance as well, its source the relationship between the man and his work. To his sympathizers, he was, as one said when Hemingway died, "a man who lived it up to write it down." To his antagonists, what he wrote obscured rather than revealed the truth about the man. Gertrude Stein, for example, disenchanted with her former protégé, wrote in 1933 that she would love to read the "real story of Hemingway, not those he writes, but the confessions of the real Ernest Hemingway . . . but alas he never will. After all, as he himself once murmured, there is the career, the career."[2] Both observers are myopic because they fail to perceive arbitrary and necessary distinctions between the life and the work. It is certainly true that at times (especially in the thirties) the "career" became outrageously disproportionate to the work, as if an excess of adventure compen-

---

[1] See Robert O. Stephens, *Hemingway's Non-Fiction* (Chapel Hill: U. of North Carolina Press, 1968), especially Chapter 5, on Hemingway as a feudist.

[2] *The Autobiography of Alice B. Toklas* (New York: Modern Library, 1933), pp. 216–17.

sated for a paucity of art. And the work too is sometimes self-conscious and postured; as Edmund Wilson remarked, Hemingway is "the worst invented character to be found in the author's work."[3] Nevertheless, it should become clear that as Hemingway projects his world, his public and literary images fuse kaleidoscopically. The perspective becomes myriad, but always there is a wholeness, an organic interdependence that suggests, as Malcolm Cowley wrote more prophetically than he knew in 1944, "a sense of an inner and an outer world that for twenty years were moving together toward the same disaster."[4]

From the outset, Hemingway's characters are vised in a world of natural and human violence, struggling to survive and to assert the integrity of self. The conflict is intense, the rules of battle merciless and strictly enforced. Love, war, and sports (usually bloody ones) are the games his heroes play and, in conventional terms, lose. From the earliest stories to the latest, the hero ends as victim. "All stories, if continued far enough, end in death," Hemingway writes in *Death in the Afternoon,* "and he is no true story teller who would keep that from you" [122].

Love, war, and sports were Hemingway's life games too, played vigorously and tenaciously from his youth. Like his protagonists, he suffered physical as well as emotional scars and, like them, tried to manifest "grace under pressure."[5] The beginnings were deceptively undramatic. One of his high-school teachers in the then prosperous, middle-class Chicago suburb of Oak Park wondered some years ago "how a boy brought up in Christian and Puritan nurture should know and write so well of the devil and the underworld."[6] Similarly naïve Midwesterners drift through the pages of Hemingway's fiction, inevitably missing the point of their experiences. Yet Hemingway's eighteen years in Oak Park were not on the surface hellish.

Ernest Miller Hemingway was born July 21, 1899, the second of six children. His mother made the boy practice the cello; his

---

[3] "Hemingway: Gauge of Morale," in Wilson's *The Wound and the Bow* (Boston: Houghton Mifflin, 1941), p. 226. Reprinted in *Ernest Hemingway: The Man and His Work,* ed. J. K. M. McCaffery (Cleveland: World, 1950), p. 245.

[4] Introduction to *The Viking Portable Hemingway* (New York: Viking, 1944), p. xxiv.

[5] The first printed reference to this famous expression appears in Dorothy Parker's profile of Hemingway in *The New Yorker* (Nov. 30, 1929, p. 31). At the close of her wide-eyed, infatuated essay, Miss Parker tells of someone at a party challenging Hemingway to define "guts." He replied, "I mean grace under pressure."

[6] Quoted in Charles Fenton's *The Apprenticeship of Ernest Hemingway: The Early Years* (New York: Farrar, Straus, and Young, 1954), p. 2.

father taught him to fish and to shoot. Nothing hinted at trauma. At high school, class of 1917, he was a prototypically zealous and competitive all-American boy: good student, all-around athlete (swimmer, football player, riflist, and, privately, a student at the local boxing gymnasium), debater, cellist in the school orchestra, editor of the school newspaper, *Trapeze,* and contributor of stories (that already hint at his mature style) and poems to the literary magazine, *Tabula.* He went off occasionally on hitchhiking trips, and once even hid himself from the law after shooting a blue heron on a game preserve.[7] To some critics, Hemingway's expeditions away from home attest to the normality of his boyhood; to others they symbolize his early rebellion against the norms of Oak Park and reflect the tensions of his home life.

Certainly his parents had sharply divergent interests that stirred ambivalent responses in him and some antagonism toward one another. Marcelline Sanford, a sister two years his senior but raised as Hemingway's twin, testifies that her parents "loved each other deeply," but admits that they "frequently got on each other's nerves."[8] A Congregationalist and obsessively religious woman (she named her four daughters after saints) but also an artistic one,[9] Grace Hall Hemingway shaped a home environment rather like a church-organized cultural salon. Clarence Edmonds Hemingway, a prominent physician and an ardent, disciplined sportsman and amateur naturalist, introduced his son to the excitement of the out-of-doors. During summers at their lakeside house near Petoskey in northern Michigan, Dr. Hemingway occasionally took his son along on professional visits across Walloon Lake to the Ojibway Indians; more often they fished and hunted together. Their bond was close, though the father was a strict disciplinarian and even more rigid and Puritanic than Mrs. Hemingway.

What each of his parents transmitted to him is at least superficially clear. His appetite for the out-of-doors and the discipline and courage of the athlete never abated. Neither did his love for music (though he hated having to study the cello) and the arts. He cherished Bach and Mozart, stressing what he had learned about writing from "the study of harmony and counterpoint"; and, he added, "I learn as much from painters how to write as from

---

[7] Hemingway wrote a long story, "The Last Good Country," about this experience. Nick Adams and his sister are the main characters.

[8] Marcelline Hemingway Sanford, *At the Hemingways: A Family Portrait* (Boston: Atlantic, Little, Brown, 1962), p. 195.

[9] She had some professional success as a singer and as a painter.

writers."[10] Nothing in the available data of Hemingway's boyhood and adolescence in Oak Park augurs other than a reasonable expectation of a well-adjusted adulthood. Yet when one turns to the fiction of this extraordinarily autobiographical writer, one notes several Nick Adams's stories written about those years ("Indian Camp," "The Doctor and the Doctor's Wife," "The End of Something," "The Three-Day Blow," "The Battler," and "The Killers") that record patterns of violence and fear, confusion and disillusion—and loneliness, the quality his classmates coupled with his versatility as most characteristic of him.

Two months before his graduation, the United States had entered the war. "College, war, and work were the choices that confronted him," Carlos Baker writes, and Hemingway's choice was work. Defective vision in his left eye made war an unlikely experience anyhow. In October 1917, he began an assignment as a cub reporter on the *Kansas City Star,* then one of the best American newspapers. For six months he covered hospital and police-station beats, absorbing also excellent professional advice from the *Star's* fine editor, C. G. (Pete) Wellington.[11] At the *Star,* Hemingway learned for the first time that style, like life, must be disciplined. "Use short sentences," read the *Star's* famed style sheet "Use short first paragraphs. Use vigorous English. Be positive, not negative." Within a remarkably short time, Hemingway learned to transmute journalistic rules to literary principle.

But the war became increasingly tempting to Hemingway,[12] and in late May of 1918 he began that adventure. Of the first two months he spent in Italy as a volunteer Red Cross ambulance driver, he was at the front for only a week. Just after midnight at the end of that week, while passing bars of chocolate to Italian soldiers at Fossalta di Piave in northeastern Italy, Hemingway was hit by fragments of an Austrian trench mortar shell. The soldier beside him was killed, another just beyond badly wounded. As he

[10] Quoted from George Plimpton's interview with Hemingway in *The Paris Review,* 18 (Spring 1958), 74. See Emily Watts, *Ernest Hemingway and the Arts* (Urbana: U. of Illinois Press, 1971). She argues that his knowledge of painting was deep rather than broad, and that his favorite painters—especially Goya and Cézanne—shared his attitudes toward life and art.

[11] The short story "God Rest You Merry, Gentlemen" and the vignette in *in our time* about two policemen gunning down two Hungarians grew out of Hemingway's apprenticeship on the *Star.*

[12] "I was an awful dope when I went to the last war," Hemingway wrote to Maxwell Perkins (May 30, 1942). "I can remember just thinking that we were the home team and the Austrians were the visiting team." Quoted from Carlos Baker, *Ernest Hemingway: A Life Story* (New York: Scribner's, 1969), p. 38.

dragged the wounded man to a rear area, Hemingway was hit in the knee by machine-gun bullets; by the time they reached sanctuary, the wounded man was already dead. At the hospital in Milan where he spent the next three months, Hemingway underwent a dozen operations to remove most of the more than two hundred shell fragments lodged in his legs and body. When he was hit, Hemingway was two weeks short of his nineteenth birthday.[13]

Early in the 1950's Hemingway said, "Any experience of war is invaluable to a writer. But it is destructive if he has too much."[14] The explosion that shattered Hemingway's body metaphorically penetrated his mind too. There its effects were longer-lived and more far-reaching. One immediate effect was insomnia and a total inability to sleep in the dark. Five years later, living in Paris with his wife, Hemingway could still not sleep without a light on. The sleepless man appears everywhere in Hemingway's fiction. Jake Barnes in *The Sun Also Rises,* Frederic Henry in *A Farewell to Arms,* Nick Adams, Mr. Frazer in "The Gambler, the Nun, and the Radio," Harry in "The Snows of Kilimanjaro," and the old waiter in "A Clean, Well-Lighted Place" are among those who suffer insomnia and dread the dark.

"After all, it's only insomnia. Many must have it," says the old waiter. Insomnia is a symptom of the agonizing syndrome that tormented Hemingway, his protagonists, and ("Many must have it") his fellow man. In a brilliantly reasoned psychological analysis of Hemingway's personality, Philip Young argues that the trauma of his war wound released more emotion than he could rationally control. Repeatedly and obsessively in his later years, Hemingway sought analogous experiences to exorcise that trauma or, failing that, by continually reliving the event through his writing rather than thinking about it, to control the anxiety it evoked.[15]

---

[13] After he was released from the hospital in Milan, Hemingway spent a few more weeks at the front in the Italian infantry—until the Armistice. He returned home in January 1919. C. Baker, *Life,* pp. 44–46, corrects several errors in the popularly accepted version of Hemingway's war experiences recounted in Malcolm Cowley's "A Portrait of Mister Papa," *Life,* 26 (Jan. 10, 1949), 86–101. Reprinted in McCaffery, pp. 34–56. Hemingway's long and amusing letter about his wound was reprinted in his hometown newspaper; see Leicester Hemingway, *My Brother, Ernest Hemingway* (New York: Fawcett, reprint, 1963) and Marcelline Sanford, pp. 166–69.

[14] Quoted in Fenton, p. 61.

[15] Philip Young, *Ernest Hemingway: A Reconsideration* (New York: Harcourt, Brace & World, 1966), pp. 164–71. Unless otherwise noted, all succeeding references to Young are to this edition.

Hemingway wrote bitterly to General Lanham (May 23, 1953) that a study (Young's) was being published trying to prove that he was "spooked" and spent all his time acting otherwise to hide the truth. In the foreword to this book, Young

Hemingway's art, not his trauma, is the ultimate concern, as Young wisely admits. Yet, within limits, Young's theory of personality helps to reconcile the man and his work. Furthermore, it lends special significance to Hemingway's observations about war and the artist. What made his war experience "invaluable" was more than the splendid recording in *A Farewell to Arms* and several short stories of the social, emotional, and ethical implications of war: it burned into his psyche a vision of man's fate that afterwards seared almost everything he wrote. The fragmenting trench mortar became a synedoche for the destructive force of a violent world, and Hemingway and his protagonists symbols of wounded mankind searching for some way to survive. He was almost ready to translate that sense of life into literature.

During the five years after he acquired his red badge of courage, Hemingway worked slowly but purposively toward his career as a writer. Oak Park welcomed its hero enthusiastically, but Hemingway's parents—especially his mother—lost patience with a young man who showed no ambition beyond writing and who seemed too willing to let the family provide for him. For a while, Hemingway wrote features for *The Toronto Daily Star* and *Star Weekly.* Shortly after his twenty-first birthday, his sister Marcelline writes, his mother issued an ultimatum that he find a regular job or move out.[16] Hemingway moved out, to Chicago, and worked for a year as editor of *The Cooperative Commonwealth,* a house organ for an investment co-operative. That winter, he met Sherwood Anderson, his first important literary acquaintance, and, through Anderson, other members of the "Chicago Group." At the same time, he met and fell in love with Hadley Richardson, a beautiful redhead, eight years older than he. Hemingway and Hadley were married in September 1921, honeymooned at the family cottage, then left for Toronto, where he continued for a few more months as a feature writer.

---

recounts his difficulties in getting Hemingway to grant permission to use quoted materials from his writing. See also C. Baker, *Life,* pp. 490 ff., for an account of the obstacles Hemingway set in the path of Charles Fenton when he was working on his study of Hemingway's formative years.

[16] Sanford, pp. 304–6. Leicester Hemingway, a younger brother, corroborates Marcelline's testimony that Hemingway's relations with his parents were strained after he returned from the war. His determination to write seemed to them irresponsible, and his first published stories shocked their Victorian sensibilities. Occasional "reconciliations" occurred, but the rupture, at last, was permanent. Leicester records that when their mother died in 1951, Hemingway sent their sister "a note and money, asking that she take everyone to dinner in his name, and tend to everything else that was necessary" (p. 247).

But it was Europe and leisure to write that he really wanted. Boldly, the Hemingways determined to chance a part-time journalistic assignment abroad. For the next two years, Hemingway became the *Star's* roving European correspondent, headquartered in Paris but filing by-lined reports of international conferences at Genoa and Lausanne, and taut, dramatic dispatches about the Greco-Turkish War. Also, he wrote casual but sharply observed impressions about skiing in Switzerland, bullfighting in Spain, and postwar life in Germany. The technique of the cable— compressed, tense—now worked even more potently on a style already affected by his earlier journalistic training, as well as by a disposition for terseness.

Meanwhile, he worked at his fiction and poetry, trying without success (as he had since 1918) to find a publisher to accept one of his pieces. In 1922, a rapid succession of events quickened his hopes and then plunged him into despair. Armed with a letter of introduction from Sherwood Anderson, he had presented himself and his writing to Gertrude Stein, whose salon in rue de Fleurus was the artistic hub of expatriates like Ezra Pound, James Joyce, and Ford Madox Ford. Stein liked the young man with the almost Continental manner and "passionately interested" eyes and encouraged him as a writer, warning him, however, that he should give up journalism altogether and rewrite his prose more economically: "There is a great deal of description in this and not particularly good description. Begin over again and concentrate." Ezra Pound, too, liked the newly arrived writer, walked and boxed with him, and urged him to go on with his poetry. In May and June, Hemingway's first published work appeared—a two-page satirical fable, "A Divine Gesture," and a four-line poem, "Ultimately," the latter printed to complete a page that featured a six-stanza poem by William Faulkner. *The Double Dealer,* a New Orleans magazine, had printed both works, and once more he owed his good fortune to Sherwood Anderson.

The disaster occurred late in 1922 while he was covering the peace conference at Lausanne. En route to meet him there, Hadley was to bring a suitcase in which she had packed nearly all his manuscripts (a few others were in the mail). At the Gare de Lyon in Paris, she left the suitcase unguarded in her compartment for a few moments and returned to find it gone. Years later, Hemingway wrote to Carlos Baker that the episode pained him so that he "would almost have resorted to surgery in order to forget it."[17]

[17] Carlos Baker, *Hemingway: The Writer as Artist* (Princeton: Princeton U. Press, 1952, 1956; 3rd ed., enlarged, 1963), p. 12 and *n.* See also Hemingway's account in *A Moveable Feast,* pp. 73–75.

With no alternative, Hemingway started afresh, this time with startling success. In 1923, several of his pieces were accepted. Harriet Monroe took six short poems for *Poetry* (published in January 1924);[18] Margaret Anderson and Jane Heap accepted for *The Little Review* (April 1923) six of the eighteen sketches that would appear in January of the following year as *in our time;* and Robert McAlmon published Hemingway's first book in the summer of 1923, *Three Stories and Ten Poems* (the stories were "Up in Michigan," "My Old Man," and "Out of Season").

However assured the future seemed, real obstacles blocked the way. Hadley was pregnant and the Hemingways had almost no money. They agreed to return to Toronto for two years, where he would earn enough money to return to Paris, and then do nothing but write. Thus they left Paris in August 1923. John Hadley ("Bumby") Hemingway was born in October, but by January 1924 the Hemingways had returned to Paris and Montparnasse, settling into an apartment in rue Notre Dame des Champs. Again the steps toward success were delayed because Hemingway had to continue working part-time to support his family. He avoided the sybaritic life of Montmartre, nearly starved himself, as he tells in *A Moveable Feast,* but kept at his writing. He was, as Gertrude Stein observed, "very earnestly at work making himself a writer."[19]

The breakthrough came in 1925—probably because two influential supporters made it possible. Even before he met Hemingway, Scott Fitzgerald had been impressed by what Edmund Wilson had shown him of Hemingway's writing and had urged Maxwell Perkins at Scribner's to ask for more. Perkins wrote, but through a series of delays and mailing errors, his letter arrived ten days after Hemingway received and accepted from Boni and Liveright, Sherwood Anderson's publishers, an offer of a two-hundred-dollar advance for *In Our Time,* a collection of short stories which included the earlier sketches published as *in our time,* and an option on his next two books.[20]

Financially, *In Our Time* was a failure, as was its successsor, *The Torrents of Spring,* a satirical parody of Sherwood Ander-

[18] George Antheil, the composer, also arranged for the publication of four poems in a German periodical, *Der Querschnitt* ("Cross-Section") in 1924–25.

[19] Ironically, Hemingway was able at this time to help Miss Stein by placing passages from her *The Making of Americans* in Ford Madox Ford's *transatlantic review,* which Hemingway helped to edit.

[20] The option proved extremely important since an additional clause provided that if the second book was not accepted, the publisher forfeited rights to the third. *The Torrents of Spring* was rejected, and Hemingway turned over to Scribner's his third book, *The Sun Also Rises.* Scribner's was his publisher for the rest of his career.

son's writing, but they brought Hemingway to the attention of major American reviewers like Allen Tate, Paul Rosenfeld, and Louis Kronenberger, each of whom proclaimed the arrival of a fresh new voice in American letters. Once more, however, it was Fitzgerald who spoke most forcibly about Hemingway's talent. In an essay called "How to Waste Material: A Note on My Generation,"[21] Fitzgerald attacked those writers of the Establishment—especially H. L. Mencken and Sherwood Anderson—whose "compulsion to write 'significantly' about America" was "insincere because it is not a compulsion found in themselves." The expatriate, Fitzgerald argued, had the advantage of being able to discover for himself an "incorruptible style" and "the catharsis of a passionate emotion." As his prime example of a writer who was "temperamentally new" and possessed of both qualities, Fitzgerald cited Ernest Hemingway and *In Our Time.* Fitzgerald's essay appeared in May; five months later Hemingway justified Fitzgerald's praise beyond question.

With Scribner's publication of *The Sun Also Rises* in October 1926,[22] Hemingway, not yet thirty, became an established literary figure. Sales were impressive for a first novel, and reviews were enthusiastic. Near the end of his life, Hemingway recollected these years—1921–26—celebrating in *A Moveable Feast* the dreams, the discipline, and the disasters. The dream is pastoral: the innocence of his love for Hadley; the beauty of place—Paris and the Voralberg; the affection of friends. Discipline, imaged as hunger, spurs him competitively and pitilessly toward success but also toward mastery of a literary style. Disaster is the nightmare reality that follows on the heels of success, shattering the dream and crumbling the discipline, leaving only lust, surfeit, and disillusion. Illness, physical and mental, probably intensified the sweetness and the bitterness of an aging man's nostalgia. Yet there is also a sense that Hemingway knew at last that the early period in Paris was the time when man and artist most happily merged. By the time he published *In Our Time, The Sun Also Rises,* and, by 1929, *A Farewell to Arms,* Hemingway had experienced all he needed to form his vision of man's fate and had forged a literary style absolutely expressive of it. Although his artistic development was not ended, what he was to write thereafter would, at its best, refine and polish his craft and play variations on themes he had already sounded.

What sustains the drama of the next two or three decades—

---

[21] *Bookman,* 63 (May 1926), 262–65. Collected in *Afternoon of an Author,* ed. Arthur Mizener (New York: Scribner's, 1958), pp. 117–22.

[22] See *n.* 20 above.

apart from the sequence of almost incredible episodes—is in some measure the remarkable flexibility with which Hemingway adjusted his public image to the special demands of changing times. That he could do so accounts for the mass personal appeal he generated—whether as the benign "Papa" or as the pugnacious "Champ." More absorbing, however, is the inward drama. As his fame swelled from a ripple to a torrent, Hemingway's sensibility seemed to wallow in the trough. In the early work, terror and beauty are too intimate to be stated: they are communicated only as feeling, rigidly disciplined. The artist controls the image of the man. In the later work, the delicacy of restrained feeling is often dissipated in statement that almost parodies the emotion. Therein lies the force of the inward drama. For almost as if to atone, the man overcompensates in life for his failure in art. His behavior in the real world continues to reflect his preoccupation with the tragedy of experience and his compelling need to combat the hostility of the universe, to affirm his own identity. But the actions are so obviously statements that they become—because they are so blatantly and determinedly heroic—comic, embarrassing, even at times boring. If, then, the twenties are the years of art as adventure, the thirties and forties are the years of the artist as adventurer. The vision remains unaltered; only the discipline slackens.

In the years between the publication of *The Sun Also Rises* and *A Farewell to Arms,* Hemingway, divorced by Hadley, married Pauline Pfeiffer, a former fashion editor for *Vogue.* They returned to the United States and settled in Key West, where Hemingway completed and published in 1927 his second collection of short stories, *Men Without Women.* In 1928, as he worked on the first draft of *A Farewell to Arms,* Pauline gave birth to the first of their two sons; as he revised the completed draft, he learned that his father, ill with diabetes, and depressed by economic reversals, had committed suicide, using his own father's Civil War revolver. Twenty years later, in an introduction to an illustrated edition of *A Farewell to Arms,* Hemingway wrote that he recalled "the fine times and the bad times we had in that year," but went on to note that he was "living in the book" and "was happier than I had ever been."[23]

The early thirties were a time of financial success, marital harmony, and high adventure. These were the years of duck and

---

[23] Young, pp. 60 ff., cites Hemingway's references to his father's suicide in *For Whom the Bell Tolls* and "Fathers and Sons" as further evidence of Hemingway's need to rehearse traumatic episodes of violence. C. Baker, *Life,* pp. 166–67, cites several entries about suicide from Hemingway's notebook for 1926.

elk shooting in Wyoming and Montana, of big-game hunting in Africa, and of fishing the waters off Key West and Bimini aboard his custom-built cruiser, the *Pilar.* They were also the years of the Depression. But to a nation demoralized by economic disaster, Hemingway seemed more than a Boy Scout gone berserk. The twenty-three lively but slick articles about hunting and fishing he wrote for *Esquire* magazine between 1934 and 1936 offered vicarious escape for the urban victims of a depression.[24] In Hemingway's rugged face and powerful torso, they discerned the lineaments of a hero in a time of defeated men; in the clipped rhythms of his understated prose and laconic dialogue a model for demonstrating "grace under pressure." Two non-fiction books published in these years reinforced the image. *Death in the Afternoon* (1932), a homage to the ritual of bullfighting, and *Green Hills of Africa* (1935), an account of a safari, rehearse the tragedy of man and beast but celebrate—almost desperately—the triumphant dignity of human courage.

The early thirties were also years in which Hemingway wrote relatively little fiction. During a comparable period in the twenties, Hemingway had published two novels, thirty-five stories, a parody, and several poems, in addition to a considerable journalistic production. His only major book during the first half of the thirties was *Winner Take Nothing* (1933), a collection of fourteen short stories.[25] In 1936, however, Hemingway published one of his finest stories, "The Snows of Kilimanjaro," in which he has his author hero berate himself for not writing the stories it was "his duty to write of."

From 1937 until the end of World War II, Hemingway, still the artist as adventurer, altered his mien. Beginning with Harry Morgan's dying words in *To Have and Have Not* (1937)—"One man alone ain't got . . . no bloody f——ing chance"—Hemingway and his characters sacrifice their privacy to the collective obligations engendered by world crises. On the surface at least, the Depression and the Spanish Civil War had shattered Hemingway's

[24] Other non-fiction he wrote during the early thirties includes critiques of paintings by Joan Miró, Luis Quintanilla, and Antonio Gattorno, and a few pieces of social and political analysis.

[25] The epigraph to this collection sets the tone. Aping the style of an old book of gaming rules, Hemingway suggests that, in the game of life, "the conditions are that the winner shall take nothing; neither his ease, nor his pleasure, nor any notions of glory; nor if he win far enough, shall there be any reward within himself." Although the collection contains two of Hemingway's most memorable stories—"A Clean, Well-Lighted Place" and "The Light of the World"—it includes at least one of his most forgettable, the long, rambling, and pointless "Wine of Wyoming."

long-held belief that "anybody is cheating who takes politics as a way out" of the writer's essential task: "to write straight honest prose on human beings."[26] Leftist critics had long ridiculed what they regarded as his hedonistic isolationism and welcomed the change. In fact, Hemingway had not in his fiction swerved to the left, and the road his characters travel 'is the familiar one — dangerous, lonely, its terminus a dead end. They had re-entered the world because democracy was probably better than Fascism, but though they were among men, they were not of them. The same remained true of Hemingway. Whatever wars he would engage in were to become *his* wars, and he fought them as he always had, on his own terms and for his own reasons.

Early in 1937, Hemingway went to Spain. Officially a correspondent for the North American Newspaper Alliance, he was not an impartial observer. He went into debt to buy ambulances for the Loyalists, attacked Fascism in an address before the Second National Congress of American Writers, helped to prepare the pro-Loyalist film, *The Spanish Earth* (1938), and wrote *The Fifth Column* (1938), his only full-length play, about the conflict. In 1939, at Finca Vigia ("Lookout Farm"), a hilltop house on an estate he had purchased in the outskirts of Havanna, Hemingway worked on his major novelistic statement about Fascism, democracy, and the individual, *For Whom the Bell Tolls* (1940).

A few days after the novel appeared, Pauline Pfeiffer divorced him for desertion. Within a week, Hemingway had married his third St. Louis–born wife, Martha Gellhorn, a novelist and journalist to whom he was wed for five years. For the first two years of their marriage, they served together as war correspondents in China, Hemingway filing reports for the now defunct New York newspaper, *PM.* In his dispatches, Hemingway thought a war between Japan, England, and the United States unlikely but not impossible. He added, prophetically, that war would become inevitable if Japan attacked American bases in the Pacific or Southeast Asia.

From 1942 until he was assigned to General Patton's Third Army in 1944 as a civilian correspondent for *Collier's* magazine, Hemingway sailed the *Pilar*—fitted at government expense with communications and demolition equipment—as a Q-boat, an anti-submarine vessel. Although the *Pilar* never encountered a submarine (had it done so, Hemingway's self-imposed orders were to drop grenades and short-fused bombs down the conning tower),

[26] *By-Line: Ernest Hemingway (Selected Articles and Dispatches of Four Decades),* ed. William White (New York: Scribner's, 1967), p. 183.

Hemingway's reports may have helped the navy to locate and sink several U-boats and he was decorated for his services. In England in 1944, Hemingway flew unscathed on several combat missions with the R.A.F. but suffered head and knee injuries in an automobile accident during a London blackout. Several newspapers printed his obituary, but shortly thereafter, on D-Day, at Fox Green Beach in Normandy, Hemingway went ashore to watch the action for several minutes before returning to his landing craft.

Despite his official assignment to General Patton's army, Hemingway attached himself to the Fourth Infantry Division of the First Army[27] and saw action during the liberation of Paris and the Battle of the Bulge. Although his accounts of his own boldness and valor are either exaggerated or distorted,[28] Hemingway did behave more like a soldier than like a correspondent. He served effectively as a scout and an interrogator at a post outside Paris, gathering intelligence for General Leclerc's advancing army. At even greater personal risk, he fought with small arms in a fierce encounter in Huertgen Forest during the German counter-offensive. Military men regarded him more favorably than did his fellow journalists. Perhaps his brashness offended them, or his lavish tales of having liberated the Travellers Club and the Ritz Hotel with a personal band of partisans.[29] But a group of correspondents preferred charges that Hemingway had violated the regulations of the Geneva Convention affecting war correspondents. After a short hearing, Hemingway was exonerated, and later received the Bronze Star.

At the end of the war, Hemingway was forty-six, his image of himself as a battered but unbowed veteran no longer a pencil sketch but a full-scaled portrait in somber oils. What remained? By statement and by action, Hemingway indicated his commitment to a fresh start in life and art. During the war years, he had

[27] It was here that Hemingway met Colonel Lanham and began a friendship that lasted until his death. Hemingway wrote more than a hundred letters to Lanham during the next seventeen years, all of them now housed at the Princeton University Library.

[28] See C. Baker, *Life,* pp. 393–445, for a precise account of Hemingway's wartime activities. Malcolm Cowley's narrative in "A Portrait of Mister Papa" (see *n.* 13 above) is infinitely more colorful and melodramatic, but suffers from hopeless distortions foisted on Cowley by Hemingway himself. In letters to Lanham, Hemingway makes clear that he is giving Cowley what he thinks Cowley wants, and saving the real stuff for his own use.

[29] See C. Baker, *Life,* pp. 416–17. Neither place required "liberation." Hemingway and a few friends were simply the first Americans to arrive and be welcomed. The only violence was sniper fire from a roof adjoining the Travellers Club. See *By-Line,* pp. 364–83.

published only his *PM* reports about the Sino-Japanese War and, for *Collier's,* his dispatches from the European theater of operations.[30] Now he spoke about a vast work-in-progress, a novel about war on "Land, Sea, and Air." As if to emphasize his feeling of renewal, Hemingway divorced Martha Gellhorn late in 1945 and in March 1946 returned to Finca Vigia with his fourth and last wife, Mary Welsh, another journalist, this time Minnesota-born.[31]

Across the River and Into the Trees (1950), Hemingway's first novel since 1940, was not the big one readers had been expecting. A year earlier, he had nearly died from erysipelas. Though the actual cause was an infection from a dust-scratched eye, Hemingway later enlivened the commonplace by telling how a bit of gunshot wadding had entered his eye during a duck-shoot near Venice. While hospitalized, he decided instead to write this shorter book. Circumstances rarely alter criticism and the novel suffered a harsh assault. The gentler critics thought it "tired" or were convinced that Hemingway had more to say; the others, who were overwhelmingly predominant, savaged it as a narcissistic self-parody. In his conspicuously autobiographic portrait of Colonel Richard Cantwell, Hemingway dwelled on his inevitable themes—death, loneliness, love, and courage—crystallized from his experiences of the forties. Henceforth, he plunged progressively deeper into his past, as if searching in nostalgia a cure for artistic impotence.[32] The cycle was nearly closed as the artist as adventurer became the adventurer searching once more for his art.

He returned first to the thirties, the venturesome years of big-game hunting and fishing. In 1953, he went to Africa with Mary on safari. This time, his already too often damaged body was nearly destroyed by successive airplane crashes. In the first accident, in which Mary suffered two broken ribs, Hemingway's liver and kidney were ruptured, his lower spine damaged; in the second, the next day, he suffered the worst of a dozen concussions in his lifetime (the craft was ablaze, the airplane door had jammed, and Hemingway butted the door open with his head) and additional in-

---

[30] *By-Line,* pp. 340–400.

[31] Although he spoke of the end of a marriage as a personal defeat, Hemingway divorced each of his first three wives at the close of a particular period of his life: Hadley at the end of his apprenticeship in Paris with the publication of *The Sun Also Rises;* Pauline at the end of the Spanish Civil War with publication of *For Whom the Bell Tolls;* Martha at the end of World War II. Each has a book dedicated to her: Hadley, *The Sun Also Rises;* Pauline, *Death in the Afternoon;* Martha, *For Whom the Bell Tolls;* Mary, *Across the River and Into the Trees.*

[32] Malcolm Cowley notes that Hemingway "sometimes seems to regard writing as an exhausting ceremony of exorcism" (Introduction, *Viking Portable,* p. xii).

ternal injuries. Although his luck was starting to run out, it was still running good, and Hemingway enjoyed reading his obituaries as he recuperated in a hospital in Nairobi.[33] He wrote a long account of his African experience, but all that he published was a two-part serial of second-rate journalism for *Look* magazine.

Fishing netted a better haul. Drawing upon a sketch he had written of a Cuban fisherman fifteen years earlier for *Esquire,* Hemingway recouped his literary losses with *The Old Man and the Sea* (1952), which won him the Pulitzer Prize in the same year and probably helped him to win, in 1954 the Nobel Prize in Literature. Now he pressed harder against the stubborn barrier of the past, pushing toward the twenties, when he had savored the ritual of the bullfight. In 1956, after working enthusiastically with Warner Brothers on the film version of *The Old Man and the Sea,* he went to Spain, hoping to translate the rivalry between two famed toreros, Antonio Ordóñez and Luis Dominguín, into another *Death in the Afternoon.* The product was again a two-part serialization called "The Dangerous Summer," this time for *Life* magazine (the rest of the manuscript has never been published), and again pallid, lifeless, almost dull.

There remained Paris, the Paris of the early twenties and his apprenticeship to art. Even before returning from Spain, Hemingway had begun to sift through a trunkload of notebooks from those years and to plan what would be, he told his wife in the jargon of *jai alai,* "biography by *remate,* by reflection." Unsettled by Fidel Castro's triumph when they returned, the Hemingways left Finca Vigia and moved to a large chalet in Ketchum, Idaho, where Hemingway reworked and polished his sketches. Mary Hemingway found the typescript in a blue box in his room after his death. "He must have considered the book finished except for the editing," she wrote in an article for *The New York Times.* It was published in 1964 as *A Moveable Feast.*

The ardor of writing must have been excruciating for Hemingway in 1960. Physically, he had deteriorated, the massive frame shrunken, the face worn and pained. At the Mayo Clinic, the diagnosis was ominous: hypertension as well as the possibility of diabetes (which had afflicted his father) and hemochromatosis, a rare disease that affects vital organs. Psychically, he was even worse, almost inarticulate, anxious, severely depressed—"an unsure schoolboy," Seymour Betsky and Leslie Fiedler wrote of him after a visit in November 1960 to invite him as a campus speaker at the University of Montana. By the spring of 1961, he had received

[33] Hemingway enjoyed especially a German report that his plane had crashed on Mt. Kilimanjaro. See *By-Line,* pp. 425–69.

twenty-five electric-shock treatments to alleviate his depression.[34] He had just returned to Ketchum from the Mayo Clinic after a month's stay when, on the morning of July 2, 1961, he placed the muzzles of a silver-inlaid shotgun in his mouth and pulled both triggers.

In *Islands in the Stream,* Hemingway's wounded hero, possibly dying, tells himself, "Don't worry about it, boy . . . All your life is just pointed toward it" [464]. Certainly the lure of death pervades Hemingway's adventures in life and art. But it is well to remember that Hemingway held passionately to living as well. What he writes about Paris at the end of *A Moveable Feast* is a metaphor he extended to his own life and to the lives of his characters: "Paris was always worth it and you received return for what you brought to it."[35]

---

[34] See. C. Baker, *Life,* pp. 550 ff. The most graphic account of Hemingway's final months is A. E. Hotchner's in *Papa Hemingway: A Personal Memoir* (New York: Random House, 1966). Its reliability, however, is questionable; see especially Philip Young's critique, "On Dismembering Hemingway," *Atlantic Monthly,* 218 (Aug. 1966), 45–49. Young's own account in the afterword to *Ernest Hemingway: A Reconsideration* is more measured, as is Leicester Hemingway's.

[35] *A Moveable Feast* was the first of Hemingway's works to be published posthumously. Nothing will appear, Young and Mann write in the preface to their inventory of Hemingway's manuscripts, that might "risk reduction of the author's stature." Among the recently published posthumous books—the novel *Islands in the Stream* as well as collections of apprentice journalism and of high-school fiction and poetry—little flatters Hemingway's image as an artist. Yet each of these works is welcome as an integral part of the yet unfinished story of the man and the artist. Still unpublished and vaulted (until the John F. Kennedy Library opens) are manuscripts of a complete novel *(Garden of Eden),* an incomplete one *(Jimmie Breen),* several short stories, a long account of Hemingway's stint as a game warden in Africa in 1953, poems, and letters.

John Graham

Ernest Hemingway: The Meaning of Style

Hemingway, in the opening pages of *Death in the Afternoon,* insists that he, his characters, and ultimately, his readers be aware of the active existence of persons, things, and actions. Too often, however, critics seem to accept this as meaning simply the accumulation of concrete details by a sensitive observer. Furthermore, the vitality of Hemingway's novels has been attributed to a number of factors ranging from his plots and characters to his simplicity of theme and control of language. These elements in their many aspects are, of course, contributory but are subordinate to a more constant cause: the active presentation of subject and object (observer and thing observed) and the continuous, intimate, and conscious relationship between subject and object. The characters' conscious reception of present fact (not judgment of or even response to fact) is so pervasive in Hemingway's novels that it appears to be a mode of thought for Hemingway, rather than a conscious artistic device. It is in this constant activity of sensory perception of active objects, and, still more important, in the subjects' awareness of relationship to these objects that the vitality of the writing is found.

The total effect of activity in the novels is gained by a simplicity of plot, a directness of human relations, and a basic impermanence of situation. The major circumstances are keynoted by impermanency: the hero is in a foreign land or, in the case of Santiago of *The Old Man and the Sea,* a foreign element. No matter how familiar the protagonist may be with the place, he is not expected to settle there. The characters "use" countries, hotels, cafes, and houses, but there is never a real act of possession. The reader waits for the next move. The main plot is dominated by violence of war, combat and/or erratic movement from place to place; the characters reflect these highly unstable conditions by their attention on the immediate present and by their lack of demand on the future. They are active, direct and, one might argue, uncomplicated people with an almost fatalistic acceptance of life. Since they are so uncomplicated in their relations and attitudes, more of a burden falls on the "working out" of the action if the novel is not to die for lack of physical, emotional, or intellectual life.

These elements of circumstance, plot, and character achieve their effects of total vitality cumulatively rather than constantly. On the other hand, it is the continuous and aware relation of active subjects and objects that vivifies the novel at all times. By the nature of Hemingway's plot and characters, and his idea of conflict, the "movement" of this relation takes on added importance since, because of its pervasiveness, it sustains the vitality, giving more flexibility in the presentation of the other elements. Without going into extended detail, the plots of the novels are certainly no more vivid, often less so, than thousands of others. While the subject is often war or physical combat, which by their very nature are intensively active, such subjects, even when coupled with credible participants, do not guarantee life but simply physical exercise. The characters may fade in and out of the action, emotionally alert but divorced from the source of the emotion. Hemingway, with the possible exception of some ruminations of Robert Jordan in *For Whom the Bell Tolls,* does not permit his characters to retreat so far from the facts of their existence that the reader concentrates on the emotion rather than on the motivating force.

A second negative point concerning the importance of this sustaining element of relation with the active concrete is the lack of development of Hemingway's characters. In a surprisingly brief time, Hemingway establishes character; in the first few chapters the reader learns all he is to know about the central actors, and these actors are as knowing about each other as they are ever to be. The action and relations which follow serve only as illustrative incidents which fix more firmly what was openly presented and readily grasped many pages before. There is nothing new to learn; even with the various crises, the characters simply observe. While they seem to understand what they do and what goes on about them, they never seem to assimilate this knowledge and, if they react, they do not change as a result.[1] There would be a real

---

[1] There is a prevailing doggedness, a form of passivity mixed with the major characters' acceptance of fact. They do not control their worlds but rather observe and react, accept and endure: Robert Jordan tenaciously follows orders (though admirably making the best of several bad bargains, i. e., the stolen exploder and his broken leg); Santiago does the usual and inevitable by trying to catch a fish and

danger of stagnation in the characters if they were not intimately aware of and actively connected with the active material world as well as the incidents in which they take part.

The final negative element that heightens the importance of movement is the lack of complexity in the conflicts presented in the novels. The simplicity, directness, and obviousness of the conflicts give the characters knowledge of the facts of their various situations. There is no challenge to the characters or the reader demanding extended mental activity, subtle or otherwise. The testimony of the participant's senses can be accepted as objective, if limited, fact. While such a simplicity is of value to a forward moving and well controlled narrative, it lessens the possibility of establishing tensions which will keep the novel alive and meaningful as it moves through its rises and falls. Vitality is preserved by the constant and conscious reception of more, though basically unvaried, information concerning the living world in which the characters operate.

The *constant* effect of vitality is gained by the rather obvious quick shifts (particularly within the unit of the paragraph) from one type of expression to another. The writing ranges freely and briefly through narration, description and exposition, monolog and dialog, and first, second and third persons.[2] Shifting points of view add a more organic variation to these essentially artificial devices. But the real force of life is conveyed by the *consciousness* of the relation between characters and an *active* material world. These relations may be physical, emotional or mental, active or static, and actual, potential, hypothetical, or desired.[3] They may be

---

staying with one when it is hooked; Frederic Henry has only a negative solution by continuing "the retreat" from the war after he and Catherine reject the world which has interfered; Jake and Brett continue an impossible, aimless existence in spite of the knowledge of experience. (Brett is so unstable in her relations that her "action" of sending Pedro Romero away is as much a different way of expressing her inability for real intimacy as a revelation of any basic goodness.)

There is, however, a deepening of the relations of the hero as the novels progress: Frederic and Catherine, Robert and Maria, and Santiago and the fish. But these relations have only an immediate and temporary unity, one which has no existence outside the present situation. It is difficult to take the love affairs seriously for there is never a sense of permanency, future, which, I venture, is a necessary note of love. There is a romantic conjuring up of the flames of love for a physical and emotional security in the extremely unstable conditions in which the characters find themselves; there is an active attempt at getting what life may offer before life goes.

[2] This type of activity is in a sense outside the world of the novel because it relies on the activity of the reader who is making subtle adjustments to the different types of presentation. It is not an activity within the world of the novel but rather a part of the direct process of artistic communication.

[3] In connection with the preceding note, no relation is "static" as long as there is an observer to consider the relation, and Hemingway always has a direct observer.

simple, one-directional relations, or become involved exchanges, expanding in both time and place.

This element of "movement" in Hemingway's novels can be observed even in his very brief and seemingly simple descriptions of people. In the description of the Russian, Karkov, there is a limited range of sensory perception, no present physical action on the part of the object, and a rather simple physical, emotional, and mental relation of subject to object:

> He had liked Karkov but not the place. Karkov was the most intelligent man he had ever met. Wearing black riding boots, gray breeches, and a gray tunic, with tiny hands and feet, puffily fragile of face and body, with a spitting way of talking through his bad teeth, he looked comic when Robert Jordan first saw him. But he had more brains and more inner dignity and outer insolence and humor than any man he had ever known.
>
> *For Whom the Bell Tolls,* p. 231.[4]

Even in such a seemingly ordinary paragraph there is much conscious relation and active detail. The opening statement of Robert Jordan's reminiscence first connects him with Karkov and indicates generally the atmosphere of the relations; this is emphasized by the concluding phrase *but not the place,* which also forces the question "why?," then "why not?" to become prominent. This question leads to the second which explains the first and implies, by *most intelligent* and *ever,* an act of evaluation and the passage of time. *Had . . . met* is the direct physical and social act which leads to the description of Karkov. The description is brief, rather disorderly, but ranging progressively in detail from clothing to physique to typical action. The inanimate articles are given a type of life by their relation to Karkov, by the participles *wearing* and *riding* and by the reader's action of forming a uniform from the separate pieces of clothing. The mannerism, *a spitting way of talking through his bad teeth,* presents two actions with a relation between each other and a further relation to an audience, specific and general. The concluding detail, *his bad teeth,* is connected intimately with the verb *talking* by the preposition *through* which

---

Even the "static physical," i. e., "the tree next to the house," demands an adjustment on the part of the observer. I do not wish to make too much of this point since it is not of immediate importance for the particular thesis at hand; it does, however, add one more constant to the present discussion.

[4] The editions cited in this study are *The Sun Also Rises* (New York, 1957), *A Farewell to Arms* (New York, 1929), *For Whom the Bell Tolls* (New York, 1940), *Across the River and into the Trees* (New York, 1950), and *The Old Man and the Sea* (New York, 1955), all issued by Scribner.

in itself is an "active" preposition denoting passage from one place to another. The independent clause presents an active judgment, *looked comic,* the temporal clause reveals an implied continuation of physical relation by the adverb *first. First* also anticipates the later change of Jordan's conclusion which is revealed in the next sentence, a concluding statement of Robert Jordan's opinion of Karkov. This statement has the implied comparison with other men, then a connection between Jordan and Karkov in *had ever known,* and a shift from *inner* to *outer* man.

Robert Jordan, the subject, has a definite activity here of both the senses and the judgment; his relation to the object, Karkov, is not only logically set forth but is explicitly reiterated. Action for Karkov is restricted and potential, but he is the cause of the activities of Jordan. The interplay of the content and the implications of the perception present the basis for the mental activity of the reader.

Other descriptions are more complex, expanding in time and in place and presenting reciprocal relationships. While Karkov may be considered "potential activity," Santiago is the result of the passage of time and action:

> The old man was thin and gaunt with deep wrinkles in the back of his neck. The brown blotches of the benevolent skin cancer the sun brings from its reflection on the tropic sea were on his cheeks. The blotches ran well down the sides of his face and his hands had the deep-creased scars from handling heavy fish on the cords. But none of these scars were fresh. They were as old as erosions in a fishless desert.
>
> *The Old Man and the Sea,* pp. 9–10.

The activity and unity here is one of cause and effect; the continuous action of nature and of past experience on the old man has produced the present figure. Although the old man is "doing" nothing, the involvement of the relationships (indicated by the blotches and scars, the results, which exist in the present) gives a history of past action and forces the reader to shift from one point to another for his perspective and evaluation of the scene and condition.

Both Karkov and Santiago are presented with a sufficient amount of concrete detail for the reader to gain a direct and concrete picture of the characters. The approach to Brett Ashley is, however, quite different. In the entire novel, the only static details we are given about Brett are that her hair is short and her figure slender. She is attractive. There is no attempt at *ut pictura poesis,* no set piece as in Scott or Balzac. Hemingway gives Brett "body" by suggesting to the reader a type: he reveals her in settings, attitudes, and actions that bring out a compulsive, jaded, unconventional animalism, and the reader may choose, from imagination or experience, the physical embodiment for these qualities. A pertinent quotation may be drawn from Jake's observation in a Paris scene: Jake and Bill have come up to a bar; Mike strides forward and greets Jake cheerily; the two talk socially:

> Bill had gone into the bar. He was standing talking with Brett, who was sitting on a high stool, her legs crossed. She had no stockings on.
>
> *The Sun Also Rises,* p. 78.

The point of concentration which has existed for the long evening has been broken; the reader no longer sees the relaxed Bill-Jake combination but an unsettled one of Mike-Jake. The reader's line of observation moves from Jake, one half of the original point of concentration, to Bill, the other half, who is the immediate object of Jake's vision. Bill Gorton has not waited for an introduction to Mike (who certainly makes himself conspicuous) but goes straightway to Brett, Brett who sits reigning insolently on a high bar stool. This shift uses the person we are with, Bill, to draw us closer to Brett, who has just come into range.

The shift demanded is not only a physical one but an emotional one involving change of tone. Jake, surrounded by the alcoholic garrulity of Mike, is in sharp contrast with the intimacy of the conversation at the bar. The present activity of Brett and Bill *talking,* the past activity of shifting up onto the *high* stool and of crossing her legs and the partially incompleted past action of dressing *(no stockings),* fills the paragraph with an undercurrent of physical activity contributing to the scene's vitality. A still further note of vitality lies in Jake's either intellectual or emotional disapproval of this scene, a scene which expands, reaching through the novel and presenting Brett for what she is: attractive, alcoholic, unconventional, loose and inclined to justify her activities. The reader is given the woman in her particular active relation to particular friends, places, and actions; the character and life are there, although Brett herself is not defined overtly or given a set, static description.

Within the limits of the paragraph, the unit under discussion, vitality might be achieved most easily and effectively in a scene emphasizing the relationships of human beings who were reacting to each other on a number of levels and with varying intensity. While this is true and important for complexity, Hemingway often gains surprisingly active effects with the simple relations of a human subject and an inanimate object to preserve a sense of continuous vitality and to instill an awareness of an immediate and direct contact with the physical world. In an act of seemingly casual observation, Robert Jordan's eyes shift from one point to another as he looks at the snow stretched out before the machine gun:

> The sun was bright on the snow and it was melting fast. He could see it hollowing away from the tree trunks and just ahead of the gun, before his eyes, the snow surface was damp and lacily fragile as the heat of the sun melted the top and the warmth of the earth breathed warmly up at the snow that lay upon it.
>
> *For Whom the Bell Tolls,* p. 282.

Not only is Robert Jordan aware of the existence of the snow, but the snow is in active relation to the sun, the trees, and the earth, changing before the man's gaze. The sun and the earth act on the snow, transforming it; the snow acts in relation to the trees, withdrawing from them; and the snow surface has a static relation (its position) ahead of the gun, before his eyes. The interconnected activity of the inanimate has its own life, independent of the observer yet in relation to him.

While Robert Jordan is rather passively conscious of the active snow object above, he is physically and emotionally very actively conscious of the view and of his relation to it as he lies above the bridge waiting for dawn and the attack.

> Robert Jordan lay behind the trunk of a pine tree on the slope of the hill above the road and the bridge and watched it become daylight. He loved this hour of the day always and now he watched it; feeling it gray within him, as though he were a part of the slow lightening that comes before the rising of the sun; when solid things darken and space lightens and the lights that have shown in the night go yellow and fade as the day comes. The pine trunks below him were hard and clear now, their trunks solid and brown and the road was shiny with a wisp of mist over it. The dew had wet him and the forest floor was soft and he felt the give of the brown, dropped pine needles under his elbows. Below he saw, through the light mist that rose from the stream bed, the steel of the bridge, straight and rigid across the gap, with the wooden sentry boxes at each end. But as he looked the

structure of the bridge was still spidery and fine in the mist that hung
over the stream.

For Whom the Bell Tolls, p. 431.[5]

The activity and relations here are many and varied, but the scene
is dominated by Jordan's observation of and identification with
the coming light and the hanging mist. In this fluid context, he
shifts his gaze from detail to detail and watches as the objects grow
clearer. He is acted upon (wet by the dew), reacts (feels) to a
movement (the give of the forest floor). The vividness of the activity of light and of the connection of detail with detail in a static
physical relation is ultimately dependent on the unity and vitality
of Jordan's awareness of his sense perceptions.

To emphasize this intimate connection between subject and
object, and their mutual relation to activity, Hemingway is fond
of presenting a picture of the countryside as seen by a moving
observer. Perhaps "picture" is inexact for it is rather an impression
which reveals the movements of the observer on an equal scale
with the general nature of the landscapes. The activity of the single
observer's continually changing perspectives and objects is trans-
ferred to the rather disconnected details and unifies and vivifies
them. A simple example of this approach may be drawn from the
trip that Jake and Bill take from Paris to Bayonne:

We ate the sandwiches and drank the Chablis and watched the
country out of the window. The grain was just beginning to ripen
and the fields were full of poppies. The pastureland was green, and
there were fine trees, and sometimes big rivers and chateaux off in the
trees.

The Sun Also Rises, p. 87.[6]

Here the vitality of the rich growth of the expanding vista is closely
connected to the vitality of the aware and pleased observer, and
the gain is mutually reinforcing.

An additional virtue of these travel episodes is that the action
has a consciously sought goal of a destination which aids in the
movement; "the bridge" in *For Whom the Bell Tolls* serves in a
similar capacity, generating an almost compulsive drive toward a

[5] The tactile element in this paragraph is balanced by the visual. For paragraphs
of exclusively tactile awareness, see those presenting Jordan checking his packs
(p. 48) and readying his submachine gun (p. 431).

[6] Compare Jake and Bill on the bus ride to Burguette (p. 108) and during their
walk through the beech wood (p. 120) in *The Sun Also Rises* as well as Colonel
Cantwell in *Across the River and into the Trees* (p. 14).

conclusion. The sense of conscious purpose in the activity of a character can increase the intensity of a scene, putting a particular demand on the person as, for example, during the retreat from Caporetto: Hemingway is not simply "picturing" or establishing an external world in which his characters will operate in some possible future. The character observes and records that external world because he *must* understand it.

> Crossing the field, I did not know but that someone would fire on us from the trees near the farmhouse or from the farmhouse itself. I walked toward it, seeing it very clearly. The balcony of the second floor merged into the barn and there was hay coming out between the columns. The courtyard was of stone blocks and all the trees were dripping with the rain. There was a big empty two-wheeled cart, the shafts tipped high up in the rain. I came to the courtyard, crossed it, and stood under the shelter of the balcony. The door of the house was open and I went in. Bonello and Piani came in after me. It was dark inside. I went back to the kitchen. There were ashes of a fire on the big open hearth. The pots hung over the ashes, but they were empty.
> *A Farewell to Arms,* pp. 229–230.

Here the goal of the subject is not simply one of perception or destination but of specific and necessary information. As he crosses the field to reach the farmhouse, Frederic describes the place in active terms but the description is, in a sense, accidental to his act of peering for an enemy. This farmhouse has a vital and direct significance to Frederic; it is not presented simply as a concrete detail in a landscape. The "purposeful observation" is the usual method employed for the apparently "incidental" presentation of concrete surroundings. Sometimes the description will have an immediate and specific significance; at others a very general one. This utilitarian aspect of observation is one of the strongest links between the characters and their world.

An interesting aspect of this purposeful relation between the observer and the world is the semi-professional view that the characters often take of their world as if they were evaluating it for an immediate or future specific use. The major characters often reveal a handbook view of an object, a view conditioned by their function as professional observers. Santiago looks at sky, water, and light for indications of future weather and fishing conditions. Frederic and Robert, as soldiers, consider roads, bridges, and terrain in terms of men, movement, and equipment, though Frederic Henry does so with a dull and jaded eye while Robert Jordan is always interested and often pleased; finally, Jake, the newspaper man, views spectacles in the colorful manner that might be expected of a journalist and sojourner. These special variations of purposeful observation are the results of two basic conditions of the Hemingway protagonists that elicit the consciousness of particular or professional knowledge. The hero is often a foreigner; even though he may know the language fluently, he is in some way an outsider, not really in the stream of tradition or daily life. As a result he must learn rather consciously as much as possible about the alien world if he is to deal with it; terrain and customs must be assimilated. Furthermore, while the hero's senses are alerted in his learning process, he, as a "professional," has something to teach the other characters, whether it be bull fighting, warfare, fishing, or eating and drinking. The hero as either student or teacher needs to be aware of the world around him—persons as well as places and things—if he is to survive as a personality and, often, as a physical entity.[7]

The final example of a presentation of the inanimate is an extremely carefully worked out picture of the bull corral in *The Sun Also Rises.* An orderly inter-weaving of concrete detail and of the crowd's restrained activity carries the observing party from the ticket gate to the top of the wall; the simple, direct narration of activity and the orderly expanding description are such that

[7] These teacher-learner relations function not only within the world of the novel but extend to the reader. The two premises—hero as foreigner and hero as professional—encourage the reader's identification with the protagonist as learner as well as submission to his (teacher's) knowledge and experience. The reader is inclined to identify himself with the hero-foreigner since the reader himself is a stranger who accepts and welcomes information given by the author (either directly or indirectly), the presentation of which he would find obtrusive under other circumstances. This attitude is not limited to acceptance of fact, but after conditioning the reader to accept him as guide to the facts of the situation, the author is in a more authoritative position in any statement he makes or impression he conveys. In some particular sphere, however, the author is often knowledgeable. The "teaching" aspect in Hemingway's novels may be divided into three basic facets: 1. Characters teach characters: Jake teaches Brett about bullfighting (Ch. XIII), peasants teach Bill how to drink wine from a skin (Ch. XI), Karkov teaches Robert Jordan his politics (Ch. XVIII), Robert Jordan teaches gun placement and observation (Ch. XXII & XLIII); 2. Hemingway teaches reader directly: Aficion, *The Sun Also Rises* (Ch. XIII), France and tipping, *The Sun Also Rises* (Ch. XIX), and fishing methods, *The Old Man and the Sea;* 3. Hemingway teaches reader indirectly: Jake prepares trout (Ch. XII), Santiago prepares fish (p. 47), and Jordan makes a bough bed (Ch. XX) and loads a gun (Ch. XLI). James B. Colvert, in "Hemingway's Morality in Action," *American Literature,* XXVII (1955), 384, quite rightly argues that Hemingway's women are all "students" of the heroes, and references to Hemingway's concern for professional knowledge and attitude may be found in Joseph Beaver, "Technique in Hemingway," *College English,* XIV (1952–53), 325–328 and Charles A. Fenton, "No Money for the Kingbird: Hemingway's Prizefight Stories," *American Quarterly,* IV (1952), 839–850. I believe the major problem in *Across the River and into the Trees* is that the teacher-learner attitude is grossly out of control.

neither could have existence (to say nothing of meaning and vitality) without the order. The eye does not stop at the top of the wall; the area is opened and expands up and out to the horizon, gathering more details and more aspects of life, in particular, people who are in turn focusing their gaze toward the center of the scene.

> "Look up there," I said.
> Beyond the river rôse the plateau of the town. All along the old walls and ramparts people were standing. The three lines of forti-fications made three black lines of people. Above the walls there were heads in the windows of the houses. At the far end of the plateau boys had climbed into the trees.
>
> *The Sun Also Rises,* p. 138.[8]

Just as the composition of a painting directs the viewer's eye to rest or to follow a certain direction, so this place, the first-person narrator, and Hemingway's description urge the reader to move from one concentric ring to another. It is as if the viewer were a sentient stone sending out ripples in a pool, aware of the expand-ing circles and the movement of points (i.e., people) on them.

Until this stage the examples considered have been of rela-tionships of persons, places, and things. These relationships have been active, significant, and recognized by the observer. The em-phasis has been on the concrete fact rather than on incident. The following examples have been chosen as examples of action but they are more than that alone; the combination of narration and description does not make the distinction of "descriptive unit" or "narrative unit" simple and clearcut. But then this is just one more of the devices for integrating all aspects of the life presented in the novels.

Within the context of the regular plot of the novel, there will be many incidents of subordinate actions contributing toward the whole. To drive the point further, parts of incidents are again subordinate actions contributing to their particular whole. Ob-viously this can be pushed back to the sentence or phrase or even word, each element being filled with actual or potential movement. The extent to which the writer "packs" his action scenes is, of course, dependent on the precise effect he wishes to achieve, but Hemingway's tendency is toward gaining as much internal action as possible and relating it closely to the characters.

The simplest form of action is the rather automatic perform-ance of commonplace deeds. The flat economy of this narrative

[8] Compare the view from the bus in *The Sun Also Rises* (p. 108).

or type can achieve a variety of effects, especially when used for contrast, but more significantly the act described is the narrator's attempt to get out of his unrecognizable emotions, to establish contact with the non-self. The drained Jake retreats to San Sebastian after the fiesta:

> I unpacked my bags and stacked my books on the table beside the head of my bed, put out my shaving things, hung up some clothes in the big armoire, and made up a bundle for the laundry. Then I took a shower in the bathroom and went down to lunch. Spain had not changed to summertime, so I was early. I set my watch again. I had recovered an hour by coming to San Sebastian.
>
> *The Sun Also Rises,* p. 234.

Jake must "establish" himself in San Sebastian, must be consciously aware of his relation to a world just as he was aware when he and Bill walked through Paris or fished in a stream. It is a part of the self-centeredness of the Hemingway protagonist who must relate all things to himself if either self or things is to have meaning. He must make a world of conscious relation. Slowly the detachment is overcome, slowly a richness of consciousness emerges, and Jake can again enjoy as well as perceive.

> I walked around the harbor under the trees to the casino, and then up one of the cool streets to the Cafe Marinas. There was an orchestra playing inside the café and I sat out on the terrace and enjoyed the fresh coolness in the hot day, and had a glass of lemon-juice and shaved ice and then a long whiskey and soda. I sat in front of the Marinas for a long time and read, and watched the people, and listened to the music.
>
> *The Sun Also Rises,* p. 235.

The world and Jake's orderly relation to it have been reasserted. The impersonality is gone, and Jake can contact only the life he wishes and come alive. The actions of the subject, the passage of time, the sights, sounds, tastes, and the transition from the heat of the day to the cool of the evening all fill this paragraph with a leisurely movement of quiet consciousness.

To the relaxed action of this scene an interesting contrast is the animal vigor and pleasure of Rafael, the gypsy, as he walks toward Robert Jordan, who has just killed a cavalry man and is setting up a machine gun in anticipation of discovery and attack:

> Just then, while he was watching all of the country that was visible, he saw the gypsy coming through the rocks to the left. He

was walking with a loose, high-hipped, sloppy swing, his carbine
was slung on his back, his brown face was grinning and he carried
two big hares, one in each hand. He carried them by the legs, heads
swinging.

For Whom the Bell Tolls, p. 474.

Not only is his walk animated but his whole body is working: arms,
hands, face. Even the dead rabbits are a part of the action as they
swing in the gypsy's grasp.

As satisfying as these presentations may be in their movement,
restraint, and solidity, one turns with interest to the presentation
of violent actions such as that of the bull's entrance in *The Sun
Also Rises:*

I leaned way over the wall and tried to see into the cage. It was
dark. Some one rapped on the cage with an iron bar. Inside something seemed to explode. The bull, striking into the wood from side to
side with his horns, made a great noise. Then I saw a dark muzzle and
the shadow of horns, and then, with a clattering on the wood on the
hollow box, the bull charged and came out into the corral, skidding
with his forefeet in the straw as he stopped, his head up, the great
hump of muscle on his neck swollen tight, his body muscles quivering
as he looked up at the crowd on the stone walls. The two steers
backed away against the wall, their heads sunken, their eyes watching the bull.

The Sun Also Rises, pp. 138–139.[9]

The activity here is literally explosive as the bull bursts from the
dark of the cage into the sunlight of the corral. Jake's anticipatory
action establishes him as a concerned part of the scene; the herald-
ing noises prepare for the entrance; then the charging, quivering
bull dominates the picture. The bull defies the crowd; the steers
wait with frightened resignation. Except for the crowd itself, all
relationships here are active and intense and anticipate future
action.

The simplicity and directness of the lines of actions in the
examples already cited give an immediacy of impact and a quick-
paced reception of active fact. More complex devices of presentation vary and control this communication. One technique employed is the revelation by grammatical structure of separate but
concurrent actions that become mutually involved. United by no
logical relation or by cause and effect, the actions draw into
closer relation characters or things which reveal or clarify each

[9] Compare the description of the fish breaking water in *The Old Man and the Sea*
(p. 69) and *Islands in the Stream* (New York, 1970), p. 121.

other. One obvious use of this device may be observed in *For Whom the Bell Tolls:*

> Robert Jordan unrolled the bundle of clothing that made his pillow and pulled on his shirt. It was over his head and he was pulling it down when he heard the next planes coming and he pulled his trousers on over the robe and lay still as three more of the Heinkel bimotor bombers came over. Before they were gone over the shoulder of the mountain, he had buckled on his pistol, rolled the robe and placed it against the rocks, and sat now, close against the rocks, tying his ropesoled shoes, when the approaching droning turned to a greater clattering roar than ever before and nine more Heinkel light bombers came in echelons; hammering the sky apart as they went over.
>
> *For Whom the Bell Tolls,* p. 75.[10]

The two actions are channeled grammatically—Robert Jordan's dressing in the independent clauses, the planes' flight in the temporal ones. The independent clauses present a base of commonplace activity and flat rhythm from which operates the harshly poetic flight and the climactic rhythm of the dependent clauses. It is through the earthborn, the personal, the individual of the guerrilla that we approach the diabolic symbol of distant, impersonal mechanization.

Another method of involving forward pace while keeping the action immediately alive is to shift from one object to another with a real or implied shift of subject:

> The count was looking at Brett across the table under the gaslight. She was smoking a cigarette and flicking the ashes on the rug. She saw me notice it. "I say, Jake, I don't want to ruin your rugs. Can't you give a chap an ashtray?"
>
> *The Sun Also Rises,* p. 57.

Jake, the subject, looked at the count who was watching Brett; the subject momentarily and implicitly shifts from Jake to the count, the object from the count to Brett. Then Brett's action of flicking the ashes occurred; "When she saw me notice it," the subject becomes Brett, the object, Jake, and then is immediately reversed. Brett requested an ashtray in a vaguely guilty manner. The shifting of subject and object, and the limited action of the scene have combined to form a vital whole. The intimate relation of Jake and Brett, her attractiveness to other men and her awareness of

---

[10] Compare Jordan's concurrent awareness of his watch (time) and Maria in *For Whom the Bell Tolls* (p. 378).

that attraction, her carelessness and Jake's control over that carelessness, are all revealed in the conscious observations in these few lines. The significant interplay is alive and active within itself without having any direct role in a specific incident in the usual meaning of the term.

In the preceding scene, the people are conscious of themselves and of each other. A different type of consciousness, more introspective and articulated, is presented by Frederic Henry as he floats down the icy river, clinging to a heavy timber. Not only is he uncomfortably aware of the present and very much involved in it, but his thoughts range back and forth in time and place.

> You do not know how long you are in a river when the current moves swiftly. It seems a long time and it may be very short. The water was cold and in flood and many things passed that had been floated off the banks when the river rose. I was lucky to have a heavy timber to hold on to, and I lay in the icy water with my chin on the wood, holding as easily as I could with both hands. I was afraid of cramps and I hoped we would move toward the shore. We went down the river in a long curve. It was beginning to be light enough so I could see the bushes along the shoreline. There was a brush island ahead and the current moved toward the shore. I wondered if I should take off my boots and clothes and try to swim ashore, but I decided not to. I had never thought of anything but that I would reach the shore some way, and I would be in a bad position if I landed barefoot. I had to get to Mestre some way.
>
> *A Farewell to Arms,* p. 242.

The activity of the subject, both mental and physical, is continuous as is the contact with the reader. The lieutenant explains to the reader the sensation in the river and the problem of judgment, considers cause and effect, admits good fortune, fears, accounts, speculates, judges, anticipates, and then doggedly fixes his mind on getting "to Mestre some way." His is an observation and consideration of both the facts and the possibilities of the situation in which he finds himself.

This intense sense of involvement with the present action, as is quietly revealed in the foregoing quotation, is nowhere more brilliantly dramatized than in the opening scene of Chapter XXI, pp. 265ff. from *For Whom the Bell Tolls,* a section too long for inclusion here. In this incident, the vivid description and rushing action fuse into a whole in which the characters act, react, and are acted upon. After opening rather "idyllically" in the quiet peace of the morning, the sound of hoofbeats comes to Robert Jordan, anticipating the entrance of the young cavalryman. The dynamiter is caught up immediately in a three-way relation: he warns Maria, readies himself, and watches for a horseman. The rider appears and the pistol roars; the man is killed and the camp aroused to frantic activity.

The section is vivid, economical, and controlled. To consider just a part of it:

> He reached his hand down toward the scabbard and as he swung low, turning and jerking at the scabbard, Robert Jordan saw the scarlet of the formalized device he wore on the left breast of his khaki blanket cape.
>
> Aiming at the center of his chest, a little lower than the device, Robert Jordan fired.
>
> The pistol roared in the snowy woods.
>
> *For Whom the Bell Tolls,* p. 265.

The brillance of the movement, detail, and sound merge to give a piercing sensory impression. The simplicity of *the pistol roared in the snowy woods* has been prepared for in every respect: the quiet country setting with the snow melting and falling is shattered by the harsh shot ringing from the heavy automatic pistol held in both hands. The idyllic is broken by the ugly; we knew both existed but their juxtaposition gives us the drama. Both of these elements are picked up again as the scene is worked out; the cavalryman is dragged through the snow, the horse tracks are a matter of concern, and Robert Jordan nervously comments on the pistol and lanyard, as he reloads. The entire section is the perfect example of the union of vital parts in a living frame to produce a dramatic and significant reality. All facets previously discussed have been integrated in this passage.

There are three factors which have been examined in this study: one, the object which is under observation; two, the subject, who, in one way or another, does the observing; and three, the nature of the relation between subject and object. Because of the usual integration of these three aspects, it has been unnecessary and impossible to prescind too sharply from any two. The conclusions reached from these discussions are briefly: the activity of the object and subject may be either physical, emotional, or mental. These activities may be presented as actual, potential, hypothetical, desired, past, or implied. The relation of the subject and object is most often one of conscious or effective recognition by one or more of the senses; the subject often seeks to observe the object for a specific, sometimes necessary, purpose. (The reader, acting as external subject, must make subtle adjustments to varying types of expression.) The sense of immediacy in Hemingway's novels is gained not by the reproduction of the object for itself or even in the perception of the object by the subject so much as by the subject's awareness of his act of perception and the activity of the object perceived.

These are pedestrian facts by way of conclusion. The actual use of this view gives a concretely interrelated world to which the characters continually testify as present *now* and accounts for Hemingway's particular achievement in such vivid scenes as the fishing trip in *The Sun Also Rises.* Depending little on the cataloging of static details in the manner of Zola and Norris, Hemingway constructs the connection of character and action which always enlivens and solidifies the characters and humanizes scenes and actions. Before, and below the level of, the formation of the Hemingway "code"—his ideal of actions, courage, endurance, and technical competency—lies the involvement with and awareness of the material and interrelated world and of the characters' recognition of that active world. This constant movement gives the novels their vitality.[11]

[11] Since this study was first issued [in 1960], I should direct the reader to Earl Rovit's *Ernest Hemingway* (New York, 1963), especially chapters II and VI which contain a number of fruitful applications and developments of some points expressed in my article. See also C. P. Heaton, "Style in *The Old Man and the Sea,*" *Style,* IV (1970), 11–27.

E. M. Halliday

Hemingway's Ambiguity: Symbolism and Irony

I

One of the curious things about *The Old Man and the Sea* was the sense of awe that it created in its author, its publisher, and (to judge by many of the reviewers) its readers. "Don't you think it is a strange damn story that it should affect all of us (me especially) the way it does?"[1] wrote Hemingway to one of *Life's* editors. And Scribner's dust jacket responded like a good Greek chorus, "One cannot hope to explain why the reading of this book is so profound an experience."[2]

There has always been a certain mystery about Hemingway's effects in his best writing. From *In Our Time* (1925), with its puzzling "chapters" connecting (or separating) the stories, through *For Whom the Bell Tolls* (1940), with its oddly equivocal interpretation of the Spanish civil war, his best has evoked a somewhat doubtful sound from critics who nevertheless were at pains to recommend. Something, it was felt, was being missed; or if not missed, then sensed too vaguely for critical description. *A Farewell to Arms* (1929), declared Edward Hope in the New York *Herald Tribune,* was "one of those things—like the Grand Canyon —that one doesn't care to talk about."[3] Despite such reverent throwing up of hands by early critics many things were aptly observed; but the emphasis was heavily on Hemingway the realist, whose bright fidelity to the perceptible surfaces of life was accomplished through living dialogue and a prose finely engineered to the accurate rendering of sensuous experience. And the brilliance of his reflected surface together with the roughness

[1] Quoted in *Time,* LX, No. 9, 48 (Sept. 1, 1952).
[2] *The Old Man and the Sea* (New York, 1952).
[3] Quoted on the flyleaf of *A Farewell to Arms,* Bantam Edition (New York, 1954).

of the things he preferred to write about—fishing, hunting, skiing, bull-fighting, boxing, horse-racing, and war—perhaps made it difficult to see one of the cardinal facts about Hemingway: that essentially he is a philosophical writer. His main interest, in representing human life through fictional forms, has consistently been to set man against the background of his world and universe, to examine the human situation from various points of view.

Not that he has a "system," for on the final questions Hemingway has always shown himself a skeptic. "It seemed like a fine philosophy," Jake Barnes says to himself at one bitter point in *The Sun Also Rises*. "In five years . . . it will seem just as silly as all the other fine philosophies I've had."[4] Like Jake, Hemingway has been "technically" a Roman Catholic, but the metaphysical doctrines of Christianity seem never to have taken a convincing hold. His most devout characters are only devoutly mystified by the universe: both Anselmo, the good old man of *For Whom the Bell Tolls,* and Santiago, of *The Old Man and the Sea,* disclaim their religiosity, and their Hail-Marys are uttered mechanically enough to evoke a chilly memory of the sleepless waiter in "A Clean, Well-Lighted Place," who prayed, "Hail nothing, full of nothing, nothing is with thee."[5] The parable of the doomed ants on the burning log, in *A Farewell to Arms,*[6] has been thought to represent Hemingway's *Weltanschauung* at its most pessimistic; but there is no reason, actually, to think that there has since been a fundamental change in his view of life. "Everything kills everything else in some way."[7] reflects the old Cuban fisherman of the latest book; and even the small bird that rests momentarily on his fishing line may fall to the hawks before reaching land, at best must take its chance "like any man or bird or fish."[8] The world, it seems, still breaks everyone, and only the earth and the Gulf Stream abide after the vortex of human vanities has subsided forever.

Given Hemingway's suspicion of ultimate doom and his passionate fondness for being alive, it is no surprise that his philosophical preoccupation is primarily ethical. Extinction may well be the end of all, as the writer of Ecclesiastes repeatedly remarked, but for Hemingway and his heroes this merely emphasizes the need to live each moment properly and skilfully, to sense judiciously the texture of every fleeting act and perception. The focus is con-

---

[4] *The Sun Also Rises* (New York, 1926), p. 153.
[5] *The Short Stories of Ernest Hemingway* (New York, 1938), p. 481.
[6] *A Farewell to Arms* (New York, 1932), p. 350.
[7] *The Old Man and the Sea,* p. 117.
[8] *Ibid.,* p. 61.

duct: "Maybe if you found out how to live in it you learned from that what it was all about,"[9] says Jake Barnes. It is not accidental that the French existentialists have shown a strong feeling for Hemingway's work. Like them he has been poised in his hours of despair on the edge of nothingness, the abyss of nonmeaning which confronts most of the characters in the stories of *Winner Take Nothing* (1933); and like them he has looked in his hours of hope to a salvation built out of individual human courage around a code, at once rational and intuitive, of strict, often ritualistic behavior. *"Nous sommes foutus . . . comme toujours,"* says Golz, the Loyalist general commanding the attack with which Jordan's mission is co-ordinated in *For Whom the Bell Tolls. ". . . Bon. Nous ferons notre petit possible."*[10] As it was for Socrates and Jeremy Taylor, although for quite different reasons, dying well is for Hemingway the crucial corollary to living well. So Robert Jordan fights off an impulse to kill himself to end the anguish of a badly broken leg and avoid possible capture. "You can do nothing for yourself but perhaps you can do something for another,"[11] he tells himself; yet we are to understand that he has died well not just because of his sacrifice, but because he has not abandoned the principle of fortitude. In the image of the crucifixion which has haunted Hemingway from "Today Is Friday" (1926) to *The Old Man and the Sea,* it is the unique courage of the forsaken and crucified man-God that takes his attention. "I'll tell you," says a Roman soldier in the earlier work, "he looked pretty good to me in there today."[12] We are part of a universe offering no assurance beyond the grave, and we are to make what we can of life by a pragmatic ethic spun bravely out of man himself in full and steady cognizance that the end is darkness.

II

Undoubtedly Hemingway's preoccupation with the human predicament and a moral code that might satisfactorily control it, in itself partly accounts for the sense of hidden significance which many have experienced in reading him. Obscured as this preoccupation has been by his choice of particular fictional materials and by his manner, which has always eschewed explication, it could

[9] *The Sun Also Rises,* p. 153.
[10] *For Whom the Bell Tolls* (New York, 1940), pp. 428, 430.
[11] *Ibid.,* p. 466.
[12] *The Short Stories,* p. 457.

nevertheless almost always be felt: it was impossible to avoid the impression that this writer was dealing with something of final importance to us all. Like the Elizabethans whom he evidently loves, he never lets us quite forget that death awaits every man at some turn perhaps not far along the way. And like nobody but Hemingway—that is, in his peculiar and distinguished manner as an artist—he continually reminds us that (as he expressed it once to Maxwell Perkins) it is our "performance en route"[13] that counts for good or bad.

But what is the essence of his peculiar manner? It is a manner of implication, clearly, as he himself has said in various notes of self-criticism of which the figure in *Death in the Afternoon* is perhaps the most striking: "The dignity of movement of an ice-berg is due to only one-eighth of it being above water."[14] The question is what mode of narrative technique he exploits in order to make the ice-berg principle operative in his work. I do not remember seeing the word "symbolism" in critical writing about Hemingway before 1940, nor have I seen more than one review of *The Old Man and the Sea* that did not lean heavily on the word. The number of exegeses that explain Hemingway as a symbolist has increased geometrically since Malcolm Cowley suggested in 1944 that he should be grouped not among the realists, but "with Poe and Hawthorne and Melville: the haunted and nocturnal writers, the men who dealt in images that were symbols of an inner world."[15] It was a startling and pleasing suggestion. Mr. Cowley advanced it rather tentatively and did not press his discovery very far; but it was taken up with something like a hue and cry by other critics who, it seemed, had been testily waiting for the scent and were eager to get on with the hunt. Literary conversation soon began to reflect the new trend: I recall hearing it asserted on two proximate occasions that the sleeping bag in *For Whom the Bell Tolls* is an "obvious" symbol of the womb; and that a ketchup bottle in "The Killers" patently symbolized blood. By 1949 it was no great surprise to open an issue of the *Sewanee Review* to an essay by Caroline Gordon called "Notes on Hemingway and Kafka."[16] It would have been surprising only if the analysis had not hinged on a comparison between the two writers as symbolists.

Is Hemingway genuinely a symbolist? I think he uses certain techniques of symbolism, but I think he does so in a very limited and closely controlled way, and that failure to recognize the con-

---

[13] Quoted by Perkins in *Scribner's Magazine*, LXXXI, 4 (March, 1927).

[14] *Death in the Afternoon* (New York, 1932), p. 192.

[15] Introduction to *The Portable Hemingway* (New York, 1944), p. vii.

[16] *Sewanee Review*, LVII, 214–226 (Spring, 1949).

trols leads—already has led—to distortions of his meaning and mis-appreciations of his narrative art. As a sample, Miss Gordon's essay is instructive on this point. Starting calmly, as her title suggests, with the assumption that Hemingway is a symbolist, she proceeds to compare him, not very favorably, with Kafka. And it turns out that Hemingway's trouble is simple—he is not *enough* of a symbolist: "this plane of action is for him a slippery sub-stratum glimpsed intermittently. It does not underlie the Naturalistic plane of action solidly, or over-arch it grandly, as Kafka's Symbolism does."[17]

But this is mistaking an artistic discipline for a fault. Hemingway has not attempted Kafka's kind of symbolism and fallen short: it is something foreign to Hemingway's art. The Kafka story used by Miss Gordon as the basis for her comparison is "The Hunter Gracchus," a carefully elaborated allegory revolving around the life of Christ—that is to say, there are two distinct and parallel narrative lines, the primary, which operates within the confines of a more or less realistic world, and the secondary, which operates within the realm of religious myth and in this case is assumed by the author to be a prior possession on the part of the reader. Incidentally, Miss Gordon forces her comparison from both sides, claiming for Kafka, as something he shares with Hemingway, "a surface which is strictly Naturalistic in detail."[18] But this claim must rest on a curious understanding of the phrase "in detail" since the story on the "Naturalistic" level offers, among other attractions, a corpse that is mysteriously still alive, and a German-speaking dove the size of a rooster.

Hemingway, as far as I know, has never written an allegory—notwithstanding the bright interpretations of *The Old Man and the Sea* that illuminated cocktail parties a few years ago when it was published in *Life*—and for a very good reason. In successful allegory, the story on the primary level is dominated by the story on the secondary level, and if the allegorical meaning is to be kept clear, its naturalistic counterpart must pay for it by surrendering realistic probability in one way or another. A strain is imposed on the whole narrative mechanism, for mere connotative symbolism will not do to carry the allegory: there must be a denotative equation, part for part, between symbols and things symbolized in order to identify the actors and action on the allegorical level. The extreme difficulty of satisfactorily conducting the dual action throughout a prolonged narrative is classically illustrated by *The Faerie Queene* and by *The Pilgrim's Progress*. The allegorist who

[17] *Ibid.,* p. 226.
[18] *Ibid.,* p. 222.

admires realism is constantly pulled in two directions at once, and is very lucky when he can prevent one or the other of his meanings from unbalancing him.

Still, Hemingway has used the symbolism of association to convey by implication his essential meaning from the time of his earliest American publication. It may well be that this was inevitable for a writer starting out with Hemingway's determination to communicate, as he put it (in *Death in the Afternoon*) "what really happened in action; what the actual things were which produced the emotion that you experienced."[19] Nothing could more clearly differentiate Hemingway's kind of realism from Zolaesque naturalistic description than this early statement of intent. Everything is to depend on judicious discrimination of objective details: *what really happened* is not by any means everything that happened; it is only "the actual things . . . which produced the emotion that you experienced." As a matter of fact "produced" is a little too strict, as Hemingway demonstrates again and again in *The Sun Also Rises* and *A Farewell to Arms,* where he depends heavily on the technique of objective epitome—a symbolist technique, if you like—to convey the subjective conditions of his characters. The details selected are not so much those which *produce* the emotion as those which epitomize it; it is the action of the story which has produced the emotion. Thus at the crisis of *The Sun Also Rises,* when Jake Barnes presents Brett to Pedro Romero—a Pandarism for which he is obliged to hate himself—his agonized feelings are not discussed, but are nevertheless most poignantly suggested by the perceptions he reports:

> When I came back and looked in the café, twenty minutes later, Brett and Pedro Romero were gone. The coffee-glasses and our three empty cognac-glasses were on the table. A waiter came with a cloth and picked up the glasses and mopped off the table.[20]

In *A Farewell to Arms,* Frederic Henry goes dully out for breakfast from the Swiss maternity hospital where Catherine Barkley is fighting for life in ominously abnormal labor:

> Outside along the street were the refuse cans from the houses waiting for the collector. A dog was nosing at one of the cans.
> "What do you want?" I asked and looked in the can to see if

[19] *Death in the Afternoon,* p. 2.
[20] *The Sun Also Rises,* p. 194.

there was anything I could pull out for him; there was nothing on top but coffeegrounds, dust and some dead flowers.

"There isn't anything, dog," I said.[21]

There is, of course, a larger sense, germane to all good fiction, in which Hemingway may be said to be symbolic in his narrative method: the sense which indicates his typical creation of key characters who are representative on several levels. We thus find Jake Barnes's war-wound impotence a kind of metaphor for the whole atmosphere of sterility and frustration which is the *ambiance* of *The Sun Also Rises;* we find Catherine Barkley's naïve simplicity and warmth the right epitome for the idea and ideal of normal civilian home life to which Frederic Henry deserts; we find the old Cuban fisherman in some way representative of the whole human race in its natural struggle for survival. But the recent criticism of Hemingway as symbolist goes far beyond such palpable observations as these, and in considering the fundamental character of his narrative technique I wish to turn attention to more ingenious if not esoteric explications.

Professor Carlos Baker, in *Hemingway: The Writer as Artist* (1952), has established himself as the leading oracle of Hemingway's symbolism. His book is, I think, the most valuable piece of extended Hemingway criticism that we yet have, and to a large extent its contribution is one of new insights into the symbolist aspect of his subject's narrative method. He is sweeping: "From the first Hemingway has been dedicated as a writer to the rendering of Wahrheit, the precise and at least partly naturalistic rendering of things as they are and were. Yet under all his brilliant surfaces lies the controlling Dichtung, the symbolic underpainting which gives so remarkable a sense of depth and vitality to what otherwise might be flat two-dimensional portraiture."[22] This may fairly be said to represent Mr. Baker's major thesis, and he develops and supports it with remarkable energy and skill. I do not wish to disparage his over-all effort—he is often very enlightening—but I do wish to argue that he has been rather carried away by his thesis, and that therein he eminently typifies the new symbolist criticism of Hemingway which in its enthusiasm slights or ignores other basic aspects of Hemingway's technique.

Mr. Baker's chapter on *A Farewell to Arms* is an original piece of criticism, and it solidly illustrates his approach. He finds that

---

[21] *A Farewell to Arms,* p. 336.
[22] Carlos Baker, *Hemingway: The Writer as Artist* (Princeton, 1952), p. 289.

the essential meaning of this novel is conveyed by two master symbols, the Mountain and the Plain, which organize the "Dichtung" around "two poles": "By a process of accrual and coagulation, the images tend to build round the opposed concepts of Home and Not-Home. . . . The Home-concept, for example, is associated with the mountains; with dry-cold weather; with peace and quiet; with love, dignity, health, happiness, and the good life; and with worship or at least the consciousness of God. The Not-Home concept is associated with low-lying plains; with rain and fog; with obscenity, indignity, disease, suffering, nervousness, war and death; and with irreligion."[23] It is in terms of these antipodal concepts that Mr. Baker analyzes the semantic structure of *A Farewell to Arms,* a structure which he finds effective chiefly because of the adroit and subtle development of the correspondingly antipodal symbols, the Mountain and the Plain. He argues that from the first page of the story these are set up in their significant antithesis, that they are the key to the relationships among several of the leading characters, and that the central action— Frederic Henry's desertion from the Italian Army to join Catherine Barkley, the British nurse—can be fully appreciated only on this symbolic basis. *"A Farewell to Arms,"* he concludes, "is entirely and even exclusively acceptable as a naturalistic narrative of what happened. To read it only as such, however, is to miss the controlling symbolism: the deep central antithesis between the image of life and home (the mountain) and the image of war and death (the plain)."[24]

Clearly there is some truth in this. The "deep central antithesis" cannot be denied, I would think, by anyone with an acceptable understanding of the book. The question at issue is one of technique; to what extent, and how precisely, is the central antithesis in fact engineered around the Mountain and the Plain as symbols?

One thing is noticeable immediately: as in virtually all of Hemingway, anything that can possibly be construed to operate symbolically does no violence whatsoever to the naturalism (or realism) of the story on the primary level. Nothing could be a more natural—or more traditional—symbol of purity, of escape from the commonplace, in short of elevation, than mountains. If thousands of people have read the passages in *A Farewell to Arms* which associate the mountains "with dry-cold weather; with peace and quiet; with love, dignity, health, happiness and the good life" without taking them to be "symbolic" it is presumably because

[23] *Ibid.,* pp. 101, 102.
[24] *Ibid.,* pp. 108, 109.

these associations are almost second nature for all of us. Certainly this seems to be true of Frederic Henry: it is most doubtful that in the course of the novel he is ever to be imagined as consciously regarding the mountains as a symbol. This of course does not prove that Hemingway did not regard them as such, or that the full understanding of this novel as an art structure does not perhaps require the symbolic equation, *mountain* equals *life and home.* It does, however, point differentially to another type of symbolism, where the character in question is shown to be clearly aware of the trope, as when Catherine Barkley says she hates rain because "sometimes I see me dead in it,"[25] or when Frederic Henry says of his plunge into the Tagliamento, "Anger was washed away in the river along with any obligation."[26]

But Mr. Baker has claimed a most exact and detailed use by Hemingway of the Mountain-Plain symbolism, and his ingenious interpretation deserves closer attention. Like many other critics he is an intense admirer of the novel's opening paragraph, which, he says, "does much more than start the book. It helps to establish the dominant mood (which is one of doom), plants a series of important images for future symbolic cultivation, and subtly compels the reader into the position of detached observer."[27] He proceeds to a close analysis of this paragraph:

> The second sentence, which draws attention from the mountainous background to the bed of the river in the middle distance, produces a sense of clearness, dryness, whiteness, and sunniness which is to grow very subtly under the artist's hands until it merges with one of the novel's two dominant symbols, the mountain-image. The other major symbol is the plain. Throughout the sub-structure of the book it is opposed to the mountain-image. Down this plain the river flows. Across it, on the dusty road among the trees, pass the men-at-war, faceless and voiceless and unidentified against the background of the spreading plain.[28]

This is highly specific, and we are entitled to examine it minutely. Mr. Baker says the river is "in the middle distance" in the direction of the mountains with the image of which, as he sees it, the symbolic images of the river are to merge into one great symbol. But is the river really in the middle distance? The narrator tells us he can see not only its boulders but its *pebbles,* "dry and white in the sun." The river must, of course, flow from the mountains,

---

[25] *A Farewell to Arms,* p. 135.
[26] *Ibid.,* p. 248.
[27] Baker, *op. cit.,* p. 94.
[28] *Ibid.,* pp. 94–95.

but in the perspective seen from the house occupied by Frederic Henry, it would appear to be very close at hand—closer than the plain, and quite in contrast to the distant mountains. And this raises the question of whether the clearness, dryness, whiteness, and sunniness offered by the river are in fact artfully intended to be associated with the mountain-image and what it is held to symbolize; or, disregarding the question of intent, whether they do in fact so operate in the artistic structure. Why must the river images be disassociated from the images of the plain across which the river, naturally, flows? Because the river images are of a kind which, if they work as symbols, are incongruent with what Mr. Baker has decided the Plain stands for; they must instead be allocated to the Mountain. This is so important to his thesis that the river shifts gracefully, but without textual support, into "the middle distance," closer to the mountains.

And what of the soldiers on the road? Since they must be firmly associated with the Plain ("war and death"), it is against that background that Mr. Baker sees them in Hemingway's opening paragraph—it would not do to see them against the background of the river, with its Mountain images. But let us look again at the paragraph.

> In the late summer of that year we lived in a house in a village that looked across the river and the plain to the mountains. In the bed of the river there were pebbles and boulders, dry and white in the sun, and the water was clear and swiftly moving and blue in the channels. Troops went by the house and down the road and the dust they raised powdered the leaves of the trees.

Mr. Baker says the road is across the river, as of course it would have to be if we are to see the figures of the soldiers against the background of the plain. Hemingway does not say the road is across the river. Indeed, everything indicates the opposite arrangement: a house on a road running along the near side of the river, across which the plain stretches out to the mountains. "Sometimes in the dark," begins the third paragraph of the novel, "we heard the troops marching under the window. . . ." The truth is that a strong part of Mr. Baker's initially persuasive exegesis of the opening paragraph of *A Farewell to Arms* hangs on a reading that the written words will not support. This is not to deny that the paragraph establishes a mood of doom by its somber tone and the epitomic symbols of dust and falling leaves: what I am questioning is the over-all symbolic organization of the novel's structure in terms of the Mountain and the Plain, which Mr. Baker argues as a prime illustration of his unequivocal judgment of Hemingway as symbolist artist.

As a matter of fact, the plain presented in the opening pages of *A Farewell to Arms* is as troublesome as the river when it comes to supporting Mr. Baker's interpretation. There are plains in many countries that could well serve as symbols of emptiness, desolation, disaster, and death—we have some in the American West. But this does not appear to be that sort of plain: quite the contrary. "The plain," Frederic Henry narrates in the opening words of the second paragraph, "was rich with crops; there were many orchards of fruit trees. . . ." Mr. Baker tells us neither how these images of fertility and fruition are to fit in with "rain and fog; with obscenity, indignity, disease, suffering, nervousness, war and death," nor how we should symbolically interpret the conclusion of the sentence, ". . . and beyond the plain the mountains were brown and bare." One can easily grant that as the novel unfolds the impression of war itself grows steadily more saturated with a sense of doomsday qualities: that was an essential part of Hemingway's theme. But to what degree is this impression heightened by the use of the Plain as symbol? The simple exigencies of history prevent exclusive association of the war with the plain as opposed to the mountains, as the narrator indicates on the first page: "There was fighting in the mountains and at night we could see flashes from the artillery." Yet if Mr. Baker is right we would expect to find, despite this difficulty, a salient artistic emphasis of the Plain in symbolic association with all those images which his interpretation sets against those coalescing around the Mountain symbol.

Mr. Baker makes much of the fact that Frederic Henry, during his leave, fails to take advantage of the offer of his friend the chaplain and go to the high mountain country of the Abruzzi, "where the roads were frozen and hard as iron, where it was clear cold and dry and the snow was dry and powdery. . . . I had gone to no such place but to the smoke of cafés and nights when the room whirled and you needed to look at the wall to make it stop, nights in bed, drunk, when you knew that that was all there was."[29] Here, Mr. Baker claims, "the mountain-image gets further backing from another lowland contrast."[30] Granting the familiar association here of mountain-country with certain delectable and longed-for experiences, one would like to see, in support of the Mountain-Plain explication, a clearer identification of the contrasting, soldier-on-leave experiences, with the lowland or plain. And while

---

[29] *A Farewell to Arms,* p. 13.

[30] Baker, *op. cit.,* p. 102.

wondering about this, one reads on in *A Farewell to Arms* and soon finds Frederic Henry and Catherine Barkley in Milan, where Henry is recuperating from his wound. They are having a wonderful time. They are in love, have frequent opportunities to be alone together in the hospital room, go often to the races, dine at the town's best restaurants, and in general lead an existence that makes the most pleasant contrast imaginable to the dismal life at the front. "We had a lovely time that summer."[31] says the hero. What has happened here to the Mountain-Plain machinery? It does not seem to be operating; or perhaps it is operating in reverse, since Milan is definitely in the plain. Mr. Baker passes over these pages of the novel rather quickly, remarking that Catherine here "moves into association with ideas of home, love and happiness."[32] He seems to be aware of the difficulty, although he does not mention it as such: "She does not really [*sic*] reach the center of the mountain-image until, on the heels of Frederic's harrowing lowland experiences during the retreat from Caporetto, the lovers move to Switzerland. Catherine is the first to go, and Henry follows her there as if she were the genius of the mountains, beckoning him on."[33]

This is romantically pleasant, but inaccurate. Catherine does not go to Switzerland, but to the Italian resort village of Stresa, on Lake Maggiore. Stresa, moreover, although surrounded by mountains, is itself distinctly lowland: you can pedal a bicycle from Milan or Turin without leaving nearly flat country. Still, it can be allowed that the lovers are not free of the contaminating shadow of war until they have escaped up the lake to Switzerland and established themselves in their little chalet above Montreux. Here, again, the associations all of us are likely to make with high-mountain living assert themselves—clear, cold air; magnificent views; white snow; peace and quiet—and the hero and heroine are shown to be happily aware of these. The rain, however, which they have both come to regard as an omen of disaster, grants no immunity to the mountain; it refuses to preserve a unilateral symbolic association with the plain. Mr. Baker knows this, but does not discuss the extent to which it obscures his neat Mountain-Plain antithesis, making the point instead that "the March rains and the approaching need for a good lying-in hospital have driven the young couple down from their magic mountain" to "the lowlands"[34] of Lausanne.

[31] *A Farewell to Arms,* p. 119.
[32] Baker, *op. cit.,* p. 104.
[33] *Ibid.*
[34] *Ibid.,* pp. 104, 108.

Here again observation is fuzzy to the point of distortion: Lausanne happens to stand on a series of steep hills and is an extraordinarily poor specimen of a City of the Plain. This is clear, incidentally, without reference to an atlas, since there are several allusions to the hills and steep streets of Lausanne in the novel itself.[35] But Mr. Baker is caught up in his symbolic apparatus, and if one symbol of death (rain) has failed to stay where it belongs in his scheme (on the plain) he still is persuaded to see the topography of Switzerland in a light that will not darken his thesis.

What all this illustrates, it seems to me, is that Mr. Baker has allowed an excellent insight into Hemingway's imagery and acute sense of natural metonymy to turn into an interesting but greatly overelaborated critical gimmick. It is undeniable that in the midst of the darkling plain of struggle and flight which was the war in Italy, Frederic Henry thinks of the Swiss Alps as a neutral refuge of peace and happiness—surely millions must have lifted their eyes to those mountains with like thoughts during both World Wars. But in so far as this is symbolism it belongs to our race and culture; and if it is to be sophisticated into a precise scheme of artistic implication revolving around two distinct polar symbols, the signals transmitted from artist to reader must be more clearly semaphored than anything Mr. Baker has been able to point to accurately. I do not believe this is derogatory to Hemingway. Sensitive as always to those parts of experience that are suggestive and connotative, he used the mountain metaphor which is part of our figurative heritage to deepen the thematic contrast in *A Farewell to Arms,* between war and not-war. But nowhere did he violate realism for the sake of this metaphor; nor did he, as I read the novel, set up the artificially rigid and unrealistic contrast between the Mountain and the Plain which Mr. Baker's analysis requires.

Mr. Baker himself has summed up the sequel to his investigation of *A Farewell to Arms.* "Once the reader has become aware of what Hemingway is doing in those parts of his work which lie below the surface, he is likely to find symbols operating everywhere. . . ."[36] Mr. Baker does find them everywhere, and they not infrequently trip him into strangely vulnerable judgments. Finding an unprecedented display of symbolism in *Across the River and into the Trees* (1950), for instance, he is willing to accord that disappointing novel a richly favorable verdict: "a prose poem, with a remarkably complex emotional structure, on the theme of the three ages of man. . . . If *A Farewell to Arms* was his *Romeo*

[35] See, for instance, pp. 328, 331, 334.
[36] Baker, *op. cit.,* p. 117.

and Juliet . . . this . . . could perhaps be called a lesser kind of
Winter's Tale or *Tempest.*"[37]

III

But we are not interested so much in the narrative technique
of Hemingway's weakest work as we are in what happens in his
best. To see symbolism as the master device of the earlier novels
and short stories tends to obscure another and more characteristic
type of ambiguity which makes his best work great fiction in the
tacit mode. I mean Hemingway's irony. The extent to which the
ironic method has packed his fiction with substrata of meaning has
not yet, I think, been adequately appreciated in published criticism. And it needs to be appreciated; for irony as a literary device
is singularly suited to the view of life which Hemingway has consistently dramatized now for a quarter of our century in such manner as to distinguish him as a writer.

If you look at Hemingway's earliest American publication in a
medium of general circulation you are struck by this irony of view
and method, just as it is strikingly there in *The Old Man and the
Sea.* "Champs d'Honneur" was the title of one of six short poems
printed in *Poetry* for January, 1923:

> Soldiers never do die well;
>   Crosses mark the places—
> Wooden crosses where they fell,
>   Stuck above their faces.
> Soldiers pitch and cough and twitch—
>   All the world roars red and black;
> Soldiers smother in a ditch,
>   Choking through the whole attack.[38]

One of the most interesting things about this is the strong ironic
tension set up between the title and the verse itself; the harsh
incongruity between the traditional notion of the soldier's heroic
death and the grim reality. A tough irony of situation is also the
keynote of *In Our Time* (1925), not only as clue to the individual
meanings of most of the stories that make up the book, but as the
very principle upon which it was composed. Many readers have
tried to puzzle out a nice relationship between each story and the
narrative fragment, numbered as a "chapter," which precedes it.

[37] *Ibid.,* pp. 264, 287.
[38] *Poetry,* XXI, 195 (Jan., 1923).

But the principle in fact was irrelevance; what Hemingway did was to take the numbered sketches of *in our time* (Paris, 1924) and intersperse them with the longer stories to give a powerfully ironic effect of spurious order supporting the book's subject: modern civil disruption and violence seen against the timeless background of everyday human cross-purposes.

The ironic gap between expectation and fulfilment, pretense and fact, intention and action, the message sent and the message received, the way things are thought or ought to be and the way things are—this has been Hemingway's great theme from the beginning; and it has called for an ironic method to do it artistic justice. All of his work thus far published deserves study with special attention to this method.

I do not think, for example, that a reader must understand the symbolic pattern Mr. Baker claims for *A Farewell to Arms* in order to get the main point of the story; but unless he understands the irony of Catherine Barkley's death he surely has missed it completely. Long before this dénouement, however, irony has drawn a chiaroscuro highlighting the meaning of the book. There is from the beginning the curious disproportion between Frederic Henry's lot in the army and his frame of mind. A noncombatant, he lives in comfortable houses, eats and drinks well, makes frequent visits to a brothel maintained exclusively for officers, and has extensive leaves urged on him by a sympathetic commanding officer. Despite such pleasures he is malcontent; and the more this fact emerges the more it becomes evident that his mood is a reflection not of his personal fortune, but of the whole dismal panorama of civilization disjointed by war. His manner of narration is already ironical: "At the start of the winter came the permanent rain and with the rain came the cholera. But it was checked and in the end only seven thousand died of it in the army."[39] Healthy in body, the hero is afflicted by a paralysis of the will, a torpor brought on by too many months of living close to the war; and this is the reason for his paradoxical failure to visit the home of his friend the chaplain while he is on leave: "I myself felt as badly as he did and could not understand why I had not gone. It was what I had wanted to do. . . ."[40] Even the one constructive effort he has been regularly capable of, the performance of his duty as an ambulance officer, has begun to seem absurdly inconsequential to him: when he returns from leave he finds that his absence apparently has made no difference whatever.

As the war wears on, its grotesqueries receive more attention;

[39] *A Farewell to Arms,* p. 4.
[40] *Ibid.,* p. 13.

it begins to be felt, indeed, that they are perhaps after all indigenous to life itself, and only emphasized by war. Henry is given a protective St. Anthony by the heroine: "After I was wounded I never found him. Some one probably got it at one of the dressing stations."[41] The ambulance unit which he commands makes elaborate preparations to receive wounded soldiers during a forthcoming attack: while they are waiting—and eating cheese and spaghetti—in a dugout, an enemy shell lands squarely on top of them, thus making Lt. Henry himself part of the first load of wounded going to the rear. For this, he learns, he is to receive a bronze medal; his friend Rinaldi hopes it may be silver.

The episode in Milan, so recalcitrant to Mr. Baker's symbolist scheme, has an integral function in the ironic structure of the narrative. Recuperating far behind the lines, the hero becomes part of the incongruously pleasant civilian scene which always—to the incredulous and bitter astonishment of most combat soldiers—goes on while men die at the front. Yet to add a further ironic twist to this, there is Hemingway's satirical portrait of Ettore, the American-Italian who is a "legitimate hero" in the Italian Army. Not only does he see the social life of wartime Milan as perfectly normal, but it is clear that his view of the war as a whole is the reverse of Henry's: "Believe me, they're fine to have," he says, exhibiting his wound stripes. "I'd rather have them than medals. Believe me, boy, when you get three you've got something."[42]

Back at the front for only two days, Henry finds himself mixed up in the nightmarish retreat from Caporetto. Hemingway's famous description of this debacle is a stringent comment on the bewildering stupidity and chaos of war, but he takes the occasion to inject again a shot of special irony. With one ambulance mired to the hubs on a rainsoaked back road, Lt. Henry shoots a sergeant who, in his anxiety to keep up with the retreat, tries to get away on foot instead of staying to cut brush for the spinning wheels. The sergeant is only wounded, but he is quickly dispatched, with Henry's acquiescence, by Bonello, one of the ambulance drivers. "All my life I've wanted to kill a sergeant,"[43] Bonello says proudly; but a few hours later he too deserts, to let himself be captured by the enemy. The climax of this grim comedy is of course Frederic Henry's own desertion. Threatened with military justice akin to that he so summarily had dealt the sergeant, he dives into the Tagliamento River; and his sarcastic remarks on his would-be

[41] *Ibid.,* p. 47.
[42] *Ibid.,* p. 130.
[43] *Ibid.,* p. 222.

executioners ring with hyperironic overtones against the baffle of the earlier incident:

> I saw how their minds worked; if they had minds and if they worked. They were all young men and they were saving their country. . . . The questioners had that beautiful detachment and devotion to stern justice of men dealing in death without being in any danger of it.[44]

There are many other ironic strokes in *A Farewell to Arms,* but it is this series, identifying the activities of war with all that is brutal and meaningless in human life, that gives the novel its predominantly ironic texture. The catastrophe, Catherine Barkley's shocking death, has the ambivalent effect of partly canceling this identification while at the same time violently reinforcing the total effect of irony. It is as if the author had said, "Do not imagine that the kind of cruelty and disruption I have shown you are confined to war: they are the conditions of life itself." It is thus only at the end that the full ironic ambiguity of the title springs into view.

The title of Hemingway's other great war novel is likewise an index of its strongly ironic theme. It was strange how many reviewers and critics underweighed the epigraph from Donne and the meaningful paradox of the whole sentence furnishing the title: "And therefore never send to know for whom the bell tolls: it tolls for thee." Appraisals from both Right and Left accused Hemingway of having gone over to the other side, while certain critics less politically biased found that his theme was confused or that it had backfired. "At the center of *For Whom the Bell Tolls,*" wrote Maxwell Geismar, "there is a basic confusion of Hemingway's intention. The novel attempts to be a constructive statement on human life. Yet Hemingway's underlying sense of destruction often contradicts this."[45]

But Hemingway was not confused. As always, he wanted to show something true about human life (not necessarily something "constructive"); and he had come to take a more complex view of humanity at war then he projected in *A Farewell to Arms.* "A plague on both your houses"—the prevailing mood of Frederic Henry—has been replaced by Robert Jordan's unillusioned sense of the community of the human predicament. No man is an island, it turns out; but the storms that sweep the human continent are of such force, and the quakes that rack its surface so disruptive, that none of us can depend on better fortune than that of Jordan, who

[44] *Ibid.,* pp. 240, 241.

[45] *Writers in Crisis* (Boston, 1942), p. 81.

died making his own small and paradoxical effort to maintain its integrity. His affiliation with the Loyalists is no simple partisan allegiance; and to extend and support the hero's explicit awareness of the inevitable contradictions of his position, Hemingway poses a series of situations pregnant with irony.

Outstanding is Pilar's account of the start of "the movement" in Pablo's home town, with its unflinching report of the steadily mounting sadism which infused the execution of the local Fascists. There is a remarkable tone to this report, as if Pilar were at confession, anxious to tell the whole truth and omitting not even the most shameful details, yet seeking at the same time to make it understood how these grisly acts could have occurred among normally decent Spanish peasants. She tells how, at first, many of the peasants were sickened by Pablo's plan to flail the Fascists down between a double line of men leading to the edge of a steep cliff. But within the ironic frame of the entire episode, in relation to the book, there are lesser ironies: for it is the cowardly behavior of the Fascists themselves that brings these peasants to a pitch of mob hatred and violence equal to Pablo's inveterate cruelty.

Throughout all this the reader is never allowed to forget that it is the Loyalists who are committing the atrocities described, and that the leaders of the massacre are the very people with whom Jordan is now allied. Robert Penn Warren cites the irony of this, but he suggests that *For Whom the Bell Tolls* is not Hemingway's best novel "primarily because . . . Hemingway does not accept the limitations of his premises . . . the irony . . . runs counter to the ostensible surface direction of the story."[46] So it does—but this is the nature of irony; and this is why it is so valuable to Hemingway in his intense effort to dramatize fully the implications of Donne's epigraph in relation to the ironical self-destruction for which is civilized warfare. It is a mistake to think of *For Whom the Bell Tolls* as a document of social optimism in its intent, as opposed to the dark pessimism of Hemingway's earlier books. The darkness is relieved, deliberately, only by a faint existentialist glimmer: the general human enterprise seems very likely to end in failure, but each of us must do what he can—*"Nous ferons notre petit possible."*

It is to this end that the irony of the Loyalist massacre of the Fascists, which early in the book sets the theme of human sacrifice in a highly critical perspective, is complemented by the irony of the dénouement. For the central action—the blowing of the bridge—which is responsible for the deaths of El Sordo, Anselmo, Fernando, and, indeed, Robert Jordan, is rendered a strategic failure by the loose tongues of their comrades behind the lines.

[46] Introduction to *A Farewell to Arms* (New York, 1949), p. xxv.

To these two fundamental veins of irony many scenes provide tributary support: three may be cited as exemplary. There is the one in which Jordan reads the letters found in the pockets of a Fascist cavalryman he has just shot, and discovers he is from a Spanish town that Jordan knows well:

> How many is that you have killed? he asked himself. I don't know. Do you think you have a right to kill any one? No. But I have to. . . . But you like the people of Navarra better than those of any other part of Spain. Yes. And you kill them. Yes. . . . Don't you know it is wrong to kill? Yes. But you do it? Yes. And you still believe absolutely that your cause is right? Yes.[47]

This irony of Jordan's self-conscious ambivalence is heightened by juxtapositions of which he knows nothing. In the midst of El Sordo's great last fight, we are suddenly given a decidedly sympathetic portrait of Lt. Berrendo, second in command of the Fascist cavalry. Julian, his best friend, has just been killed by Sordo, and Captain Mora, the blustering officer in command, is shouting blasphemies at the hilltop in an effort (which carries its own small irony, in view of his imminent death) to prove that no one is left alive up there. Later, after Mora has become El Sordo's "Comrade Voyager," Berrendo reluctantly has his troopers decapitate the dead guerrillas for "proof and identification," and the Fascists start back towards their headquarters:

> Then he thought of Julian, dead on the hill, dead now, tied across a horse there in the first troop, and as he rode down into the dark pine forest, leaving the sunlight behind him on the hill, riding now in the quiet dark of the forest, he started to say a prayer for him again.[48]

At this point Anselmo, watching from a hillside, sees them ride past; and on his way back to the guerrilla cave he crosses El Sordo's hilltop where he finds the headless bodies of his comrades: ". . . as he walked he prayed for the souls of Sordo and of all his band. It was the first time he had prayed since the start of the movement."[49] The episode thus ends in ironic equilibrium, with both sides petitioning Heaven. But we have not yet seen our last of Lt. Berrendo. It is he who looms in the sights of Robert Jordan's machine gun in the last paragraph of the story, lending the finale an ironic depth that protects it from false heroics. For these two young soldiers, preponderant as our sympathy may be for one

[47] *For Whom the Bell Tolls,* pp. 303–304.
[48] *Ibid.,* p. 326.
[49] *Ibid.,* p. 327.

rather than the other, the same bell tolls. The novel is Hemingway's fullest work so far in scope and artistic realization, and to its fulfilment the ambiguity of irony contributes an essential part.

IV

It would be foolish to argue that the work of any first-rate writer owes its success exclusively or even predominantly to any one narrative artifice. Hemingway has used techniques of symbolism and techniques of irony and used them well; what we want in criticism is an even view of his use of these and other artistic resources that does not exaggerate one at the expense of others. A point deserving great attention and emphasis about this writer is his devotion to the implicit rather than the explicit mode: and both symbolism and irony truly serve this artistic purpose. Hemingway, in fact, stirs thought as to the interrelationship of these two kinds of ambiguity. It is remarkable how often they operate together in his stories: an ironic fact, perception, or event on the primary level may epitomize an irony in a broader context, and thus doubly deserve selection and accurate report by the narrator. As an illustration of his early effort to communicate "what really happened in action," Hemingway tells in *Death in the Afternoon* how he worked on the problem of accurately depicting a certain bullfight incident:

> . . . waking in the night I tried to remember what it was that seemed just out of my remembering and that was the thing that I had really seen and, finally, remembering all around it, I got it. When he stood up, his face white and dirty and the silk of his breeches opened from waist to knee, it was the dirtiness of the rented breeches, the dirtiness of his slit underwear and the clean, clean, unbearably clean whiteness of the thighbone that I had seen, and it was that which was important.[50]

Clearly, it was the startling irony of the contrast that struck Hemingway here as "important"; but certainly (if not so clearly) there is also the symbolic suggestion of another contrast going far beyond the physical—the ironically pathetic gap, perhaps, between the matador's professional failure and his untouched inner pride which is the subject of "The Undefeated."

In a fictional narrative the double operation, ironic and sym-

[50] *Death in the Afternoon,* p. 20.

bolic, can often be seen more sharply: take *The Old Man and the Sea,* where in effect the same subject is dramatized. The old fisherman's physical triumph in catching the great fish is ironically cut down—or transmuted—into spiritual triumph by the marauding sharks who leave him with only the skeleton of the largest marlin ever seen in Cuba. Without working out the metaphor in precise terms it can be said that the irony of the event itself would hardly be so effective without the broadening and deepening of its implication through symbolic suggestion.

It may be true that all perceptions are reducible finally to perceptions of likeness or perceptions of difference. Perhaps this offers a clue to the effectiveness of both symbolism and irony for a writer who, like Hemingway, makes it his life's business to tell a truth, as he once put it, "truer . . . than anything factual can be."[51] With all his famous skill in writing with his eye upon the object, he understood from the beginning that it was only the object in relationship to other objects and to the observer that really counted: significance is, in short, a matter of likeness and difference. This is to speak broadly; and to apply the generalization to symbolism and irony requires a good deal of qualification. Yet symbolism does depend essentially on likeness, and irony on difference; and as artistic tools both are means of interpreting imaginatively, and with the flexibility of implication, a complex reality. Symbolism signifies through a harmony, irony through a discord; symbolism consolidates, irony complicates; symbolism synthesizes, irony analyzes.

For all of this, I would not like to see Hemingway go down in new literary histories as either "a symbolist" or (less likely, if somewhat more appropriately) "an ironist." Taken at face value the denomination "symbolist" has meanings in the common language of criticism that are quite inapplicable to him. But beyond this, Hemingway uses symbolism, as I have tried to show, with a severe restraint that in his good work always staunchly protects his realism. So likewise does he use irony. It is the ambiguity of life itself that Hemingway has sought to render, and if irony has served him peculiarly well it is because he sees life as inescapably ironic. But if we must classify him let us do him justice: with all his skilful use of artistic ambiguity, he remains the great *realist* of twentieth-century American fiction.

---

[51] Introduction to *Men at War* (New York, 1952), p. xi.

Bern Oldsey

The Snows of Ernest Hemingway

> *"Mais où sont les neiges d'antan?"* François
> Villon, *"Ballade des Dames du Temps Jadis"*

I

It is by now no secret that Ernest Hemingway was a writer of the outdoors and that he was always interested in "the places and how the weather was." If there were a school of meteorological criticism Hemingway would be one of its favorite authors, just as the storm scene in *King Lear* would be one of its favorite scenes. Almost every serious student of Hemingway has had his say on either the weatherscape or the landscape; in his *Hemingway: The Writer as Artist* Carlos Baker combines both into a theory of gigantic symbolic enterprise. On a more modest level (in a book of simpler title, *Ernest Hemingway*) Philip Young tends to see much of Hemingway's personality and some of his artistic output in terms of a certain narrowing, or broadening, of streams—as with that section of the *Piave* where Hemingway was first wounded, or the section of the stream in "The Big Two-Hearted River," where it enters the swampy blackness. Both of these writers agree that the weather is made to count for something in Hemingway's fiction; but both feel also that the weather cannot easily be detached from the writing for analytical purposes, and have limited themselves, as have other commentators, to the analysis of mainly one section of the Hemingway weatherscape—rain—emphasizing it as portent, omen, or symbol of death and destruction.[1]

[1] See Carlos Baker, *Hemingway: The Writer as Artist* (Princeton 1952), p. 105; and Philip Young, *Ernest Hemingway,* Rinehart Critical Studies ed. (New York, 1952), p. 64.

For some reason or other, no one has listened very hard to Pablo, the guerrilla leader in *For Whom the Bell Tolls,* who announces: "We will have much snow." It is about time someone did, because his words, as Robert Jordan discovers, are accurate within the context of the novel; and they are no less accurate in respect to Hemingway's work as a whole. For snow is the single most consistent and illuminating image in that work, not rain. Even in *A Farewell to Arms,* with its numerous rainy portents, snow imagery abounds and maintains a thematic centrality; and in the Hemingway canon as a whole there is a linking together of stories and novels by snowy traceries leading from high concepts of purity to sloughs of melting disgust. If we follow Pablo's unwitting lead, we discover that snow (with its related imagery of ice, cold, cleanness, whiteness, and light) constitutes the major natural and symbolic element of Hemingway's fictional world, notwithstanding the mountain-and-the-plain pattern that has been discerned there.

Of course all climatic and topographical elements do blend together in establishing scenic and symbolic effects. But the repetitious manner in which Hemingway follows the snow image is special, compulsive, and revealing. He uses it where expected (in stories about Switzerland, for example) and at times expected (winter and late fall), but he uses it at other times (May) and in stories that do not seem to call for snow in any way particular. For instance: "She sat at the table in her bedroom with the newspaper folded open before her and only stopping to look out of the window at the snow which was falling and melting on the roof as it fell." This is the beginning of a little-known story called "One Reader Writes." Reflecting Hemingway's early interest in Ring Lardner's epistolary technique, it is told mainly through a letter from an illiterate woman to a physician who gives free advice in the newspaper. Her husband, an ex–army man, has picked up a case of "sifilus" in China. And what she wants to know is whether she can cohabit with him after he finishes taking a series of injections.

What the reader wants to know is, why snow? Why should a story of this kind—set in Roanoke, Va., no less—begin with snow? We expect it in "An Alpine Idyll" or "Cross-Country Snow" or "The Snows of Kilimanjaro." But not here. Nor do we expect it at the beginning of something called "Banal Story," which is less a story than a free-hand satire on the brand of romanticism once published in *The Forum.* Nevertheless, "Banal Story" begins: "So he ate an orange, slowly spitting out the seeds. Outside, the snow was turning to rain."

For the time being, it is enough to note that in this piece, as in "One Reader Writes," the snow is melting or "turning to rain" and there is an implied contrast between a cozily romantic view of life and cold reality. While *The Forum* warms its readers with neatly controlled materials, "twenty-one feet of snow" falls in Mesopotamia, and in Spain Manuel Garcia Maera lies "with a tube in each lung, drowning with pneumonia."

The unlooked for entry of snow is also forced into *The Old Man and the Sea.* We could hardly hope to find snow imagery in a book of this sort, which has the sea, and a semi-tropical sea at that, as its setting. But it comes—in the shape of images summoned up by the coldness Santiago experiences as he dreams of lions and white beaches and mountains in a peculiarly mixed symbolic hope of supremacy and purity. "He could not see the green of the shore now but only the tops of the hills that showed white *as though they were snow capped. . . .*" The italicized phrase makes the point: if the hills cannot be snow capped in actuality, they can be made to appear so. A literary habit, once firmly entrenched in the brain, cannot easily be re-routed.

It was a habit that began early, not only in the regular short stories but even in the satirical form of *The Torrents of Spring.* Actually this parody of Sherwood Anderson might better have been called *The Last Snows of Winter,* since the entire narrative unravels against a backdrop of omni-present snow. In this "Romantic Novel in Honor of the Passing of a Great Race," the subtitle of the book, Hemingway concentrates on the dissolution of several things—the American Indians as a race, the love affairs of Scripps O'Neil, and the sentimental manner of Anderson—in terms of the remaining snows of winter that under the chinook wind will become rivulets and slush. The novel, if it can be called that, begins twice, and in either instance with a snow scene. One of the protagonists, Yogi Johnson, stands looking out into the yard of a pump factory where "snow covered the crated pumps that would soon be shipped away," and his breath makes "little fairy tracings on the cold window pane." The other, Scripps O'Neil, begins his version in almost the same way, "looking at the snow-covered pump yards," and thinking of his two wives. Only at the very end of the book does the chinook come "to the Frozen little Northern Town," but still no torrents, actually, just a sickening thaw.

The little northern town of Petoskey, Michigan, gives way to Venice, Italy, as parody gives way to self-parody in *Across the River and Into the Trees.* This novel (1950) reads like an imagistic and symbolic travesty of "The Snows of Kilimanjaro" (1936). It is literarily encased in ice. Its very first sentence establishes the thermometric mode: "They started two hours before daylight, and at first, it was not necessary to break the ice across the canal. . . ." The third paragraph pictures the lagoon, where Colonel Cantwell is going to shoot duck, as covered with ice, which his boat shatters "like sheets of plate glass." When he shoots his first bird, he sees it fall, "a black patch on the same ice."

The first chapter of *Across the River* prefaces a sequence of flashbacks through which the narrative unfolds. The novel's icy opening and freezing penultimate scene, of the continued hunt, frame-in Cantwell's reflections on the past forty-eight hours of his life, which have been meticulously planned to provide the best of all preludes to death. How to meet death, how to prepare for it, where to be buried, how to preserve love—all these considerations are twined together in a filigree of ice and snow imagery. For example, in sending a painting to his *innamorata,* Renata, Cantwell muses to himself about the proper message: "I better just give her my love. But how the hell do you send it? And how do you keep it fresh? They can't pack it in dry ice. Maybe they can. . . ." Renata herself describes a strange dream in which she seems to ski in blackness. Asked how this is done, she answers, "It is the same runs except that it is dark and the snow is dark instead of light. . . ." The ski run in the dark and the bird as a black patch on the ice are related to Cantwell's running commentary on death. In one instance he describes the frozen corpses of soldiers in the Huertgen Forest as having fared better than those of burnt Germans eaten by cats and dogs in their own villages. "Where would you like to be buried?" Renata later asks. "Up in the hills," he says: "On any part of the high ground where we beat them."

Across the River, it finally appears, is a specious enlargement of "Kilimanjaro"—with the protagonist's life-span enlarged, and the woman exchanged for a younger girl, but with the retrospective technique and the continued concern with purified, triumphant death the same, or nearly the same, with something gone wrong in the treatment. The drake Cantwell shoots at the conclusion of the novel is meant to be as important a symbol as the frozen leopard at the beginning of "Kilimanjaro." The drake's death presages that of the Colonel himself. But at best, the presentiment is serio-comic or wryly ironic: "The drake hit with his head down and his head under ice. But the Colonel could see the beautiful winter plumage on his breast and wings." At worst, there is something ludicrous in it; the final posture presents the wrong end.

II

In his three major novels Hemingway utilizes snow-ice imagery and symbolism in varying degrees and ways. *The Sun Also Rises* focuses imagistically on the sun itself, and almost completely breaks out of the pattern here being described. But it contains one notable, gratuitous intrusion of snow and ice which becomes particularly interesting when we think of it in connection with "An Alpine Idyll" (a story in which a man keeps his wife as a frozen corpse for a winter) and Cantwell's notion about sending his love to Renata preserved in ice. Jake Barnes and Bill Gorton fish high up in the cold mountain streams; and at one point, waiting for Bill, Jake reads a book by A. E. W. Mason, containing a curious story "about a man who had been frozen in the Alps and then fallen into a glacier and disappeared, and his bride was going to wait twenty-four years exactly for his body to come out on the moraine. . . ." This vicarious incident would hardly be worth mentioning except that it acts—in Hemingway's first novel, full of imagistic *sol y sombra*—as a footnote to the later development of the love-and-death-in-the-snow motif.

Much more importantly, snow becomes the right element for love in *A Farewell to Arms.* The first chapter of this novel opens with the stylistically famous description of the dusty road in late summer and ends with the lines: "At the start of the winter came the permanent rain and with the rain came the cholera. But it was checked and in the end only seven thousand died of it in the army." Snow symbolically offsets rain in the second chapter and acts as an antidote to the filthiness of cholera, just as the character of the young priest acts as an antidote to the filthiness of the brothel. In fact, priest and snow are introduced into the novel together: "Later, below in the town, I watched the snow falling, looking out of the window of the bawdy house . . . looking out at the snow falling slowly and heavily. . . . My friend saw the priest from our mess going by in the street. . . ." This natural churchly alb is drawn out later, in the first interactive scene of the novel, when the priest, the butt of coarse jokes by fellow officers, invites Lieutenant Henry to spend his leave at his home in the Abruzzi. The other officers are scornful and advise Henry to go instead to the cities, "to centres of culture and civilization." Thus from the very outset Henry is faced by a choice between the clean snowy regions of the Abruzzi and the murky black regions of metropolitan iniquity. His choice is recorded in post-leave recollection:

> I had gone to no place where the roads were frozen and hard as iron,
> where it was clear cold and dry and the snow was dry and powdery

and hare-tracks in the snow and the peasants took off their hats and called you Lord and there was good hunting. I had gone to no such place but to the smoke of cafes and nights when the room whirled and you needed to look at the wall to make it stop, nights in bed, drunk, when you knew that that was all there was, and the strange excitement of waking and not knowing who it was with you, and the world all unreal in the dark and so exciting that you must resume again unknowing and not caring in the night, sure that this was all and all and all and not caring.

Afterward Frederick Henry admits that the priest "had always known what I did not know and what, when I learned it, I was always able to forget." The "it" is rather mysterious, but probably refers to the *chiaro* in the *chiaroscuro* and by extension to the grace and purity of certain kinds of love, for which snow, in one of its literary guises, acts as symbolic accompaniment. Eventually Henry learns "it" and does not forget it, for eventually he and Catherine Barkley find their own cold, clear, dry country. They enter Switzerland (ironically enough, "to do the winter sport") and their entire stay there is described in constant relationship to snow conditions. In Chapter 38 they set up housekeeping: "That fall the snow came very late. We lived in a brown wooden house in the pine trees on the side of the mountain and at night there was frost so that there was thin ice over the water in the two pitchers on the dresser in the morning." They find themselves living in another land like the priest's, where "the wheel ruts and ridges were iron hard. . . ." But they have not entirely forgotten Frederick Henry's former way of life: Catherine, speaking of all the girls he must have known, says (in a rueful manner reminiscent of "One Reader Writes"), "It's not a pretty picture you having gonorrhea"; and he answers, "I know it. Look at it snow now." In Chapter 39 the roads are still hard-packed with snow and every time they go out in the fine country it is "fun." But by Chapter 40 and the month of March, things have begun to dissolve and Catherine must wear heavy overshoes: "It rained on all morning and turned the snow to slush and made the mountain-side dismal." So they descend from their idyllic land to the end of everything, with the still-born child and Catherine's death. Technically speaking, what is most important in all this meteorological treatment is that the thematic choice—between formal religion and the mundane "religion" of human love—expresses itself through parallel lines of snow imagery.[2]

[2] The analysis presented here is in basic agreement with that of Robert Penn Warren in his introduction to *A Farewell to Arms,* Scribner's Modern Standard Authors ed. (New York, 1953), but differs in imagistic slant and emphasis.

The snow section of *For Whom the Bell Tolls* covers roughly 123 pages, or 11 chapters (14 to 25), and contains four very significant episodes, including one of two scenes which Hemingway himself liked best in all his output.[3] This section also contains the most explicit statement the author (through Robert Jordan) ever made about storms in general and snowstorms in particular. After Pablo's irritating prediction of *"Mucha nieve,"* Robert Jordan, frustrated at not being able to put his demolition plan into action, discovers his emotions shifting under the influence of the storm and makes this observation:

> In a blizzard, a gale, a sudden line squall, a tropical storm, or a summer thunder shower in the mountains there was an excitement that came to him from no other thing. It was like the excitement of battle, except that it was clean. There is a wind that blows through battle . . . hot and dry as your mouth. . . .
> But a snowstorm was the opposite of all that. In the snowstorm you came close to wild animals and they were not afraid. . . . In a snowstorm it always seemed, for a time, as though there were no enemies. In a snowstorm the wind could blow a gale; but it blew a white cleanness and the air was full of driving whiteness and all things were changed and when the wind stopped there would be stillness.

This is a remarkable passage. With key phrases—"excitement," "opposite of all that," "no enemies," "white cleanness," "stillness," and *"all things were changed"*—it provides some inkling as to how the weather is meant to function in Hemingway's fiction: in addition to scenic excitement it is supposed to provide psychological drama and symbolic overtones. As we shall see later, such matters are handled with varying amounts of irony and ambiguity—sometimes as signs, sometimes objective correlatives, and sometimes full-fledged symbols.

The first snow episode in *For Whom the Bell Tolls* shows old Anselmo keeping to his post in the driving snow, holding gallantly and foolishly to his orders administered by the *Inglese.* Several times he is reasonably tempted to leave: "I must go in spite of all orders for I have a report to make now, and I have much to do in these days, and to freeze here is an exaggeration and without utility." But he stays. Haunted by death-thoughts, concerned about his disloyalty to God (whom he has given over to the Falangists), he remains true to his cause and friends. When Jordan later comes to get him, he is militarily impressed and personally touched

[3] Malcolm Cowley declares this scene and El Sordo's guerrilla action as Hemingway favorites, in "A Portrait of Mr. Papa," *Ernest Hemingway: The Man and His Work,* ed. John K. M. McCaffrey (Cleveland, 1950), p. 53.

by the old man's courage and tenacity. Against Anselmo's stead-fastness is posed the treacherous changeability of Pablo, who openly declares, "With the change of the weather I am with thee." It so happens in this instance that his open declaration is a lie; but later Pablo is with them because the weather and events have changed to make it more profitable to be so.

The bad smell of Pablo, of battle, and of death is counteracted by Anselmo, by the snowstorm, and by the sleeping-bag affair in the snow. Pilar has just finished her olfactory description of death—compounded of "refuse pails," "cigarette butts," "gunny sacks," *"casas de putas,"* and "rotted blooms," to mention only the pleasanter ingredients—when Jordan decides to get outside the sickening cave and prepare his sleeping bag. His nausea dissipates in the snowy night air. Other scents, sweet and clear—"pine boughs," "fresh-cut clover," "mimosa," "coffee," "cider," and "bread fresh from the oven"—are summoned by his mind's nose as he waits for Maria. She comes "running long-legged through the snow" to the sleeping bag, in a modern version of "Saint Agnes' Eve," and together in the snow (like Catherine Barkley and Lieutenant Henry) they make their "alliance against death."

Thereafter both love and death mingle in the snow imagery of *For Whom the Bell Tolls.* Death comes quickly the next morning in the form of the fascist cavalryman: "A warm wind came with daylight and he [Robert Jordan] could hear the snow melting in the trees and the heavy sound of its falling. It was a late spring morning. He knew with the first breath he drew that the snow had been only a freak storm in the mountains and it would be gone by noon. Then he heard a horse coming. . . ." Jordan kills the approaching enemy, who is dragged through the melting snow, leaving behind a scarlet track, until his big gray horse is caught by Primitivo.

The cavalryman gets this close to the guerrilla band because of the laxness of Rafael, the gypsy, who is supposed to have been on guard, but who instead, upon hearing a "male thumping in the snow," follows the tracks of two hares high up in the snow and kills them. "You cannot imagine what a debauch they were engaged in," he tells Jordan, who had himself been engaged with Maria, whom he calls "Rabbit," in a similar enterprise. The similarity extends itself, for Robert Jordan proves later to be as unfortunate as the male hare; and his death approaches in terms of snow imagery also—"he lay very quietly and tried to hold on to himself that felt slipping away from himself as you feel snow starting to slip sometimes on a mountain slope. . . ." Thus the pattern is reinforced, with these elements once more woven thematically together: an idealized death high in the mountains, with snow acting as the purifying agent, and animals (here the hares) acting as subhuman precursors to human expiration.

III

To put things on a statistical basis, eleven of Hemingway's first forty-nine collected short stories begin with snow imagery (by comparison, only three start with rain); two others begin with white or light references; two with coldness; and three more, though not opening in this fashion, make important internal use of snow, ice, cold, white, and light imagery.[4] This means that over a third of the stories fit the pattern—a significant portion of his work, especially when added to the sum of such material discovered in the novels.

Not all the stories within the pattern stress this line of imagery to the same extent. Some use it for little more than scenic detail. "Che Ti Dice La Patria," for example, simply begins with a mentioning of snow in the distance—"On the other side were snowy mountains." The story moves away from the mountains, descending toward a rainy conclusion. Italy, in the hands of Mussolini, has fallen upon bad days; the snows are far away: this, as the title indicates, is "what your country says to you." At least this is what it says to the two visitors who in their travels note everywhere how Italy has deteriorated. "Wine of Wyoming" begins in like manner —with snowy mountains in the distance. Here again the snow has little structural or symbolic function. The story starts with the narrator-writer observing that "the mountains were a long way away and you could see their tops." He sits on the back porch of a house owned by a French-American family of bootleggers; and his dreamy staring off into the distance is interrupted by Madame Fontan, proprietress, who brings out bottles of beer and asks, "What do you see out there?" "The snow," he answers; and she adds a bit of understatement worthy of Hemingway himself: *"C'est joli la neige."* The only narrative point of contact for the snow seems to be the French family's immaculate cleanness.

[4] As tentatively categorized, these are the stories: "The Snows of Kilimanjaro," "Cross-Country Snow," "In Another Country," "Che Ti Dice La Patria," "A Simple Enquiry," "An Alpine Idyll," "Banal Story," "God Rest You Merry, Gentlemen," "One Reader Writes," "Homage to Switzerland," "Wine of Wyoming"; "Hills Like White Elephants," "A Clean, Well-Lighted Place"; "A Day's Wait," "A Pursuit Race"; "The Light of the World," "A Way You'll Never Be" (at the end), and "The Gambler, The Nun, and the Radio" (less importantly). If taken in its *Death in the Afternoon* form, "A Natural History of the Dead" can be added to the first grouping.

Snow gains narrative importance in something like "Homage to Switzerland," which—along with "Banal Story" and *The Torrents of Spring*—is a parody in snow time. Here the object of satire is neither *The Forum* nor Sherwood Anderson's sentimental outpourings, but the stiffly formal travel literature one finds in Swiss travel folders or *The National Geographic*. "Homage" has three parts and three main characters—Messrs. Wheeler, Johnson, and Harris. All are American, all have had something go wrong with their lives, and all are waiting for the Simplon-Orient Express, which is late. Mr. Wheeler, who abhors women, waits at Montreux. The first paragraph of his section begins: "Inside the station café it was warm and light"; and ends: "Outside the window it was snowing." To kill time Mr. Wheeler amuses himself by playing a dirty trick on his waitress: knowing there is no time or place in which to do it, he offers her an exorbitant price "for a thing that is nothing to do" (as she sees it). The second and third sections make use of incremental repetition—both beginning with the warm station café and the snow outside the window, though at Vevy and Territet respectively. It is as though Switzerland had standard, interchangeable towns and the story standard, interchangeable parts, with certain modifications. In Part II Johnson tries to ease the pain of recent divorce by talking about it with new-found drinking companions. In Part III Harris, discussing the National Geographic Society with an old Swiss gentleman, eventually blurts out the fact that his father has committed suicide—"Shot himself, oddly enough." In each of the three parts, snow, along with the almost antiseptic cleanness of Switzerland, is made to act as an ironic complement to psychic wounds that have come unbound.

Certainly "Homage" is a strange story, but no more strange than "One Reader Writes," which immediately precedes it in the canon, or "A Day's Wait," which immediately follows. This last, to be best appreciated, should be read as a companion piece to "God Rest You Merry, Gentlemen." Both are from *Winner Take Nothing* (1933), both concern youths with mistaken medical notions, and both utilize wintry settings to cast an odd white light over physical suffering.

"God Rest You Merry, Gentlemen" opens with the narrator, a reporter, walking back to the municipal hospital, located on a hill overlooking Kansas City. He has partaken of Christmas food and cheer with some confrères at a bar; his mood is quietly merry, enhanced by the falling snow and the sight, in a dealer's window, of a car "finished entirely in silver with Dans Argent lettered on the hood." When he reaches the hospital, however, his slightly bacchic mood dissolves as he listens to the story told by Drs. Wilcox and

Fischer. It seems that through Wilcox's mishandling of matters a boy has performed an amputation under the misapprehension that he was castrating himself and thus curing himself of a terrible lust, a sin against purity and "our Lord and Saviour." As a result, the boy may die from loss of blood on Christmas day. The pristine snow, the chaste car (with its radiator device of a silvery dancer), and the boy's mistaken concept of purity almost blend into a successful representation of a strangely pagan-Christian conflict. *Almost,* because like a number of Hemingway's secondary works this fails to focus properly, and any commentary trying to provide the necessary synthesis would be forced.

"A Day's Wait" does better. In fact, this is one of the most unjustly overlooked of Hemingway's short pieces. With the quiet horror of childhood, it comes close to Henry James' "Turn of the Screw," and has the advantage of succinctness. It begins: "He came into the room to shut the windows while we were still in bed and I saw he looked ill. He was shivering, his face was white. . . ." The "he" in this instance is a nine-year-old boy whose nickname is Schatz; he has contracted a mild case of influenza and runs a temperature of a hundred and two Fahrenheit. Having heard in school that "you can't live with forty-four degrees," he believes he is going to die; he believes this for an entire day and night, until finally his father discovers his fear and is able to explain the difference between Fahrenheit and Centigrade: "Poor old Schatz. It's like miles and kilometers. You aren't going to die." Finally the boy is convinced—"But his gaze at the foot of the bed relaxed slowly. The hold on himself relaxed too, finally, and the next day it was very slack and he cried very easily at little things that were of no importance." During the day's wait, after administering the prescribed drugs and trying to read aloud to the boy, the father goes out for a while:

> It was a bright, cold day, the ground covered with a sleet that had frozen so that it seemed as if all the bare trees, the bushes, the cut brush and all the grass and the bare ground had been varnished with ice. . . . We flushed a covey of quail under a high clay bank. . . . Some of the covey lit in trees, but most of them scattered into brush piles and it was necessary to jump on the ice-coated mounds of brush several times before they would flush. Coming out while you were poised unsteadily on the icy, springy brush they made difficult shooting. . . .

This more than Currier and Ives sketch—of master, dog, and quail —is somehow the precise counterpoise, or imagistic correlative, needed in balancing off the feverish boy back in his room believing himself in death's grip.

There are other Hemingway stories besides "A Day's Wait" and "God Rest You Merry" that group themselves on a basis of snow-white-light imagery. "In Another Country," "An Alpine Idyll," and "Cross-Country Snow" are three of those which (along with "One Reader Writes") begin with snow and revolve around marital problems. Edmund Wilson and others have pointed out the battle of the sexes apparent in "The Doctor and the Doctor's Wife," "The End of Something," "The Three-Day Blow" (here and elsewhere the weather or topography functions in the battle), "Cat in the Rain," "Out of Season," "Cross-Country Snow," etc. All of these show the male and female ego in battle, or as in "The End of Something" at battle's end. In this respect, "Big Two-Hearted River" can be read as a retreat not only from the concussion of actual warfare but also from the world of women; it forms a fitting conclusion to *In Our Time* and a suitable transition to Hemingway's next collection of stories, entitled appropriately enough *Men Without Women* which carries on the line of retreat, the farewell to female arms, in such pieces as "In Another Country," "Hills Like White Elephants," "Ten Indians," "A Canary for One," "An Alpine Idyll," and "Banal Story." One of the stories in *Men Without Women,* "A Simple Enquiry," leads to the inevitable question of homosexual gratification.

"In Another Country" is a bitterly ironic piece that turns on the sad predicament of an Italian major, a war hero, a real "hunting-hawk," who unlike the American narrator has really earned his medals. The title, taken from Marlowe's line in *The Jew of Malta,* applies to a wench who is dead, but in this case the beautiful and beloved wife of the major. He married her only after he himself had been "safely invalided out of the war," but she dies shortly afterward of pneumonia. Part of the effect of the story is obtained through the opening paragraph, which represents the good, clean death in the snow: "It was cold in the fall in Milan and the dark came very early. Then the electric lights came on, and it was pleasant along the streets looking in the windows. There was much game hanging outside the shops, and the snow powdered in the fur of the foxes and the wind blew their tails. The deer hung stiff and heavy and empty, and small birds blew in the wind and the wind turned their feathers." The entire story is implicit in this opening: the dark does come early; there has been a certain kind of hunting; the men are stiff and empty; and the narrator later confesses to being one of the small birds, not one of the hunting-hawks.

"In Another Country" (the German title for *A Farewell to*

Arms) presents in capsule the problem faced by Frederick Henry
—why should a man marry? The answer provided by the Italian
major is the answer of hostages to fortune—a man should not marry. The same answer seems implicit, though for different reasons,
in "Cross-Country Snow." In this the snow is hard-packed and
good for skiing, though in several places soft enough to trap both
Nick Adams and his friend George into a spill. These two mascu-
line refugees from the world of women cannot quite escape the
problem of marriage and the loss of freedom that pregnancy and
children represent. They frolic about as snowy *wunderkind* themselves: we see George's big back and blond head "faintly snowy"
as he skis "hissing in the crystalline powder snow. . . ." He and
Nick ski together in a "smother of snow," "puffs of snow," and a
"wild cloud of snow." However, pregnancy and its consequent loss
of freedom for Nick, enter in the person of a waitress at the inn
where they rest and drink wine. Their talk about bumming across
the "Oberland and up the Valais and all through the Engadine"
comes to a halt when George abruptly asks, "Is Helen going to
have a baby?" Nick admits that his wife is pregnant and that he
wants the baby no more than does the unmarried waitress whose
presence has reminded them of his own situation. All that George
and Nick have left is the "run home together."

"An Alpine Idyll" is almost a continuation of "Cross-Country
Snow," or a slightly altered retelling. For George and Nick, Hemingway has substituted John and an I-narrator; they too have
stopped at an inn after skiing; they are waited on by a waitress (this
one not pregnant); and in comfortable surroundings they hear
from an innkeeper and sexton what a peasant named Olz has done
to his dead wife. "An Alpine Idyll" ends all thought of Hemingway's having consistently used either snow, the freezing state, or
the mountains as a straight symbol of purity and good life or death.
The key word in the title, the strangely applied *Idyll,* with all the
pastoral peace it implies, well illustrates his ironic application of
symbol. Here in the high country, the snow and cleanness cut
across the symbolic grain, working in mocking contrast with the
peasant brutality and coarseness of the tale. The frozen state is
itself parodied: the wife-corpse stands in the woodshed as a device
for holding a lantern (in her *mouth*) while her husband cuts wood.
"It was very wrong," the priest later admonishes the husband, and
then asks: "Did you love your wife." The answer is "Ja, I loved
her . . . I loved her fine."

Hemingway provides in his works a long string of deaths in
snowy or icy form; that in "An Alpine Idyll" stands directly opposed to the usual thought of purity-in-death implied by the dead

hares in *For Whom the Bell Tolls,* the ice-bound drake of *Across the River,* the snow-powdered foxes of "In Another Country," and the frozen leopard of "Kilimanjaro." It stands in opposition to Colonel Cantwell's idealized burial up above the timber line and Harry's post-mortem leap to the snowy crown of Mt. Kilimanjaro. In one sense it opposes, in another supplements, another Hemingway piece, which has the distinction of being framed in snow references—"A Natural History of the Dead."

Though "A Natural History" appears among the collected short stories, it comes from *Death in the Afternoon* (1932), where it is introduced by these words: "Madame, I have the very thing you need. It's not about wild animals nor bulls. It's written in popular style and is designed to be the Whittier's *Snow Bound* of our time and at the end it's simply full of conversation." What follows is much different from the relatively idyllic portrayal of life in his time by Whittier; what we get instead is a bitter naturalistic account of death and a short diatribe against the Neo-Humanists— "with their quaint pamphlets gone to bust and into foot-notes all their lust." The only connection with *Snow Bound* is a play on words: there is a burial of some corpses (including that of a fine Italian general with an eagle feather in his Alpine hat) high up in the mountains in the snow. These corpses are snow bound, or preserved, at least until spring, when the rain makes it necessary to bury them again in a less pure way. "A Natural History" ends with a conversation that reflects the disappointment of the Old Lady and, in a different sense, that of the Author. She says, "Is that the end? I thought you said it was like John Greenleaf Whittier's *Snow Bound.*" And he replies: "Madame, I'm wrong again. We aim so high and yet miss the target."

IV

Missing the target and not reaching the snow-bound state becomes the echoic theme of "The Snows of Kilimanjaro" with its post-mortem flight and epigraphic symbolism of the leopard. As one might expect, it is this central story of Hemingway's that marks his fullest utilization of snow as imagery and symbol. Once in the title, once in the epigraph, and seventeen times in the story proper the word *snow* or *snows* appears. Ten segments of the story fit the snow-ice pattern, including the all-important one that takes place in Harry's last flickering thoughts. Most of the snow imagery comes in the first sequence of flashbacks early in the story. These act as miniature forecasts or recapitulations of the kinds of incidents we have thus far discerned in works discussed: we stand waiting for the Simplon-Orient Express as in "Homage to Switzerland"; we ski on slightly crusted powder snow as in "Cross-Country Snow"; we hunt hare and see trails of human blood as in *For Whom the Bell Tolls;* we walk on snowy roads that are "sleigh-smoothed" and "urine-yellowed" as in *A Farewell to Arms.* Later we hear the sad tale of a half-wit who leaves a corpse frozen in a corral for a week in a manner reminiscent of "An Alpine Idyll." We even get an early form of Santiago's dream in *The Old Man and the Sea,* when he combines lions (here the leopard) with snowy peaks of perfection.

Once and for all, the contrasting episodes of "Kilimanjaro" should lay to rest the idea that only good things happen in the Hemingway highlands. Somewhere in the Bulgarian mountains a group of girls die in the snow, betrayed by someone named Nansen, who is either a villain or a poor weather observer.[5] On Christmas day someone named Barker flies across the lines "to bomb the Austrian officers' leave train" and returns to brag about it. And someone else named Herr Lent loses everything gambling in a snow-bound inn—"Everything, the skischule money and all the season's profit and then his capital."

Within the bounds of this single story—which is only about 9,000 words long, but has the scope of a novel—there are numerous "good" and "bad" episodes that counterbalance each other and produce effects of ambiguity or near-paradox. It is perhaps for this reason that Hemingway made the title "The *Snows* of Kilimanjaro" rather than "The *Snow* of Kilimanjaro," though the latter might have been appropriate, since what is presented in actuality is a snow-capped mountain. But the plural is much better attuned to Hemingway's ambiguous and ironic kind of symbolification. In other words, there are snows and there are *snows* (we have already seen how this is so in two such different works as *A Farewell to Arms* and *The Torrents of Spring*). The title can represent the dreamed-of snow in Harry's mind as well as the actual snow of the mountain; it can represent the destroying quality of a snow-like cloud of locusts as well as the preserving quality of Kilimanjaro's snow.

Whatever other symbolic antitheses it may subsume, the pluralized title has direct application to the extent that here in the

[5] Hemingway mixes irony with history here: the weather observer should be a good one, since he is in all probability Fridjof Nansen, the Norwegian Arctic explorer, who, for his assistance with the refugee problem after WWI, received the Nobel Peace Prize, and had named after him a certificate granted refugees by the League of Nations (a Nansen Passport).

shadow of Kilimanjaro are summoned up in Harry's mind the snows of all his yester-years. The story falls well within the *ubi sunt* category. Its five retrospective sections, *à la recherche du temps et des femmes et des neiges perdus,* owe something to Proust but more to Villon and his *"Ballade des Dames du Temps Jadis"*—with its remembrances of Flora, Thaïs, Héloise, Beatrice, and Queen Blanche; and its famous refrain of *"Mais où sont les neiges d'antan?"*[6] There are some marked similarities between the poem and the story in tone, attitude, and theme. Most of the women in Villon's poem prove the downfall of a man or men; Harry's women—including Helen and his first wife and those like the "hot Armenian slut"—have all threatened to un-man or de-man him by diverting energies that should have been applied to his writing. Thus Harry's imaginary flight constitutes the ultimate in a long line of withdrawals from female arms; part of its motivating power comes from the immemorial fear of castration.

But it is not as simple as that—even when we throw in as comparative evidence the young boy in "God Rest You Merry, Gentlemen." Though "Kilimanjaro" may be a modern variant of the Abelard theme, we find several thematic strains mixed together in snowy clusters. First, this is the story of a jaded writer who has known too many women ("Look at it snow now," says Lieutenant Henry) and is about to die artistically unfulfilled. In one sense, it stands as the naturalistic equivalent of Milton's sonnet on his blindness and Keats' "When I Have Fears that I May Cease to Be." The fear of wasted talent at mid-life lies at the bottom of all three of these otherwise different works. Hemingway looks back over what has been accomplished, or rather Harry does, and fears dying before his pen has gleaned his teeming brain, before his books can hold forth like rich refrigerators the meat of life before it rots. In this sense the story can be read as a writer's parable, a search for perfection in style and performance, with Kilimanjaro's peak a symbol of perfection.[7]

In another sense, "The Snows of Kilimanjaro" is the most complex of Hemingway's symbolic attempts to reach the heights of formal religion through secular means. In it the author comes closer than in any other of his works to achieving balance between exterior (imposed, allusive) symbol and interior (contextually

---

[6] Hemingway was certainly impressed by Villon's refrain; according to Fenton he once changed it to meet the decrease of good Negro boxers in Paris, so that it ran— *"Où sont les nègres d'antan?"* And in *Across the River,* he has Colonel Cantwell muse in true villonesque fashion— *"Où sont les neiges d'antan? Où sont les neiges d'autrefois? Dans le pissoir toute la chose comme ça. . . ."*

[7] *Cf.* Young, pp. 48–50.

derived) symbol. The symbolic intent of the story becomes immediately apparent in the epigraph, which Hemingway himself wrote to fit his narrative needs, but which (Alfred G. Engstrom has suggested) he consciously based on Dante's leopard of fleshly sins and mountain of righteousness.[8] The concern with symbolism comes through also in conversations between Harry and Helen: he tells her death need not be thought of in the form of a skull or a scythe; a buzzard, hyena, or two bicycle policemen (his own private symbol) will do just as well. Later we find death symbols in the snow-like cloud of locusts coming up from the south, and of course the snow of Kilimanjaro, which may constitute the best of all symbols for the icy purification of death, the good death.

What Hemingway provides in a lay form of art is the mythic function of purity, of grace, of absolution—long a part of man's religious hopes. Harry had come to Africa to cleanse himself of fleshly sins, to "work the fat off his soul the way a fighter went into the mountains to work and train in order to burn it out of his body." In his imagined airplane flight he goes through death (the locusts coming up from the south, like "the first snow in a blizzard") and rebirth ("then it darkened . . . the rain so thick it seemed like flying through a waterfall") to absolution and the House of God ("all he could see, as wide as all the world, great, high, and unbelievably white in the sun, was the square top of Kilimanjaro"). Admittedly, like all symbolism, this is limited and only partly valid as expression for something suprahuman and only partly conceivable. It represents, however, the efforts of a 20th-Century North American Caucasian, working with a series of primordial weather images, to arrive at a mythic solution not far removed, as the epigraph indicates, from the ancient belief of the Masai tribesmen.

In his monumental effort to trace similarities between primitive and modern archetypal manifestations, Carl Gustave Jung investigated various mythic, theological, and even alchemistic sources. Here in one of his passages dealing with the purification of the soul he utilizes a concept taken from Greek alchemy; it is hard to read the passage without thinking of it as an explanation of "Kilimanjaro":

> After the ascent of the soul, with the body left behind in the darkness of death, there now comes an enantiodramia: the *nigredo* gives way to the *albedo*. The black or unconscious state that resulted from the union of opposites reaches the nadir and a change sets in. The falling

[8] Oliver Evans ("'The Snows of Kilimanjaro': A Revaluation," PMLA, LXXVI, Dec. 1961, 603) takes exception to Engstrom's source-finding, as does Douglas H. Orrok (Modern Language Notes, LXVI, Nov. 1951, 441).

dew signals resuscitation and a new light: the ever deeper descent into the unconscious suddenly becomes illumination from above. For, when the soul vanished at death, it was not lost; in that other world it formed the living counterpole to the state of death in this world.[9]

What all this proves, of course, is not that Jung had read Hemingway, or Hemingway read Jung (although these are more than possibilities),[10] but that Hemingway was working out of an impulse toward purification and transference that has appealed to man so often as to have become an archetypal pattern.

V

Whatever archetypal patterns occurred to Hemingway's creativity, they almost inevitably associated themselves with the weather—and particularly with the line of snow-ice-cold-clean-white-light imagery we have been discussing. Although only a close study of each of Hemingway's works, with due emphasis placed on the various aspects of literary art, can give us a true estimate of Hemingway's meaning and accomplishment, an analysis of these recurrent images moves us close to what is unique in his artistic achievement. This imagistic modality provides certain clues to Hemingway's personality, ethics, esthetics, and even his slightly declining literary reputation.

The repetition compulsion set forth by Freud in *Beyond the Pleasure Principle* has already been discovered in Hemingway by Philip Young, specifically in respect to traumatic experiences attuned to death.[11] Young's theory is that shock and violence act as both cause and effect as respects Hemingway's literary productivity; and although Hemingway himself rather cryptically rejected the theory,[12] there can be little doubt that he wrote in an ever-

---

[9] *The Collected Works of C. G. Jung,* tr. R. F. C. Hill (London, 1954), XVI, pp. 279–280.

[10] Hemingway, along with Gertrude Stein and E. E. Cummings, contributed work to the monthly literary magazine called *transition;* in his *Freudianism and the Literary Mind* (Baton Rouge, La., 1957), p. 45, Frederick J. Hoffman, though making no connection between Hemingway and Jung, states that "among those who sponsored and wrote for . . . *Transition,* Jung was a favorite," because of his stand on the writer's special alliance with the unconscious. According to Eugene Jolas, Hoffman adds, "Jung was an active sponsor of *Transition.* The surrealists, on the other hand, were almost unanimously (and usually unwelcome) supporters of Freud."

[11] Young, pp. 136–143.

[12] George Plimpton, "An Interview with Ernest Hemingway," *The Paris Review,* No. 18 (Spring 1958), 69.

increasing circle of death and that most of his art consists of variations on the theme. Repetition manifests itself in the diction,
rhythms, and objective correlatives he selected to express man's
primitive condition in the face of constant death. What is addition-
ally pertinent is that he tended to see death in terms of white and
black imagery—light and the absence of light, day and night, snow
and muck, purity and impurity.

Hemingway can be caught in the act of imagistic repetition so
often that eventually the possibility of mere coincidence dwindles
to zero. Even in accounting for his own life and work he repeatedly
applied images following the snow-ice-cold pattern. In describing
his first wounding, he said, "The machine gun bullet just felt like a
sharp smack on the leg with an icy snow ball."[13] In explaining his
choice of profession, he said, "I decided, cold as a snake, to be a
writer and to write as truly as I could all my life."[14] In discussing
the circumstances under which he wrote *The Torrents of Spring,*
he said, "I wrote it after I had finished the first draft of *The Sun
Also Rises . . .* to cool out."[15] In providing an afternote for his
movie script, *The Spanish Earth,* he discusses the entire process of
making the film under the heading of "The Heat and the Cold."
And, finally, in revealing how he reached a peak of production one
day, he said:

> The stories you mention I wrote in one day in Madrid on May 16
> when it snowed out the San Isidro bullfights. First I wrote "The Kil-
> lers," which I'd tried to write before and failed. Then after lunch I
> got in bed to keep warm and wrote "Today is Friday." I had so much
> juice I thought maybe I was going crazy and I had about six other
> stories to write. So I got dressed and walked to Fornos, the old bull
> fighter's café, and drank coffee and then came back and wrote "Ten
> Indians." This made me sad and I drank some brandy and went to
> sleep.[16]

It is a moot point whether the May snow gave Hemingway "so
much juice," but it is safe to say that this unusually late snow left
its mark on his imagination since it, or one very like it, a freak
storm, turns up in *For Whom the Bell Tolls,* and accounts for one
of his favorite scenes. The fact is Hemingway never wasted a flake

[13] Charles A. Fenton, *The Apprenticeship of Ernest Hemingway: The Early Years*
(New York, 1954), p. 68.
[14] Fenton, p. 184.
[15] Charles Poore, ed., *The Hemingway Reader* (New York, 1958), p. 24.
[16] Plimpton, p. 79.

of snow; once he even did an article for *Esquire* on how to drive an automobile in heavy snow.[17]

Hemingway's creativity becomes even more clearly part of a pattern of snowy grays and whites when we consider his esthetic intent. He often admitted to learning much about literary art from the work of painters; and what he had to say of Goya, whom he admired greatly, and El Greco, whom he admired little, helps locate that intent. "Goya," he writes, "did not believe in costume but he did believe in blacks and in grays, in dust and in light, in high places rising from the plains, in the country around Madrid, in movement, in his own cojones, in painting, in etching. . . ."[18] This homage to Goya obviously sums up Hemingway's own artistic credo; and what becomes apparent is that Hemingway is best viewed as a literary etcher who concerns himself with high-lights and shadowings. When a vivid color does occasionally show up in his work it impresses us as being out of place. In this and other respects he differs from El Greco, who believed in "blues, grays, greens, and yellows, in reds, in the holy ghost, in the communion and fellowship of saints. . . ."[19] For Hemingway, the main trouble with El Greco was not that he believed in color or religion, but that he was feministically flamboyant, exhibitionistic, superfluous in his art.

Like another shaper of American prose, Henry David Thoreau, Hemingway inveighed against the superfluous and insisted on the efficacy of simplicity: "Prose is architecture," he declared, "not interior decoration, and the day of the Baroque is over."[20] The deepening effect of Thoreau's cold, clear pond is reflected in one of Hemingway's most revealing dicta: "If a writer of prose knows enough about what he is writing about he may omit things that he knows and the reader, if the writing is written truly enough, will have a feeling of those things as strongly as though the writer had stated them. *The dignity of the movement of an ice-berg is due to only one-eighth of it being above water.*[21]

By now the imagery of an ice-berg should not be surprising, as once again the repetition compulsion extends to the metaphoric. In fact, the compulsion may be more apparent than the nicety of the intended metaphor, since, it might be argued, an ice-berg does eventually melt; and if purity, dignity, and simplicity are to be part

[17] Fenton, p. 151.
[18] Ernest Hemingway, *Death in the Afternoon* (New York, 1932), p. 205.
[19] *Ibid.*
[20] *Ibid.,* p. 191.
[21] *Ibid.,* p. 192 [emphasis added].

of Hemingway's esthetics, what of permanence? A tentative answer might help explain what has been noted in those fictional episodes where snow or ice is shown to be melting. In the present reference to the ice-berg the emphasis is on dignity and the part standing for the whole. It is really an imperfect image for what Hemingway wants to say about art; but what he wants to do here is concentrate on its wholeness in frozen state, on its synecdochic conveyance of dignity. Elsewhere, as in "Banal Story," "One Reader Writes," and *The Torrents of Spring,* he concentrates on the dissolution, the impermanence of the frozen image. This is the basic paradox.

Actually, Hemingway was much concerned about the problem of achieving permanence in art forms. Bullfighting, he declared, "is only kept from being one of the major arts because it is impermanent." Only temporarily, at peaks of performance, can it even give the impression of enduring, of emulating the frozen quality of sculpture. For any art or artist the "great thing is to last" and the writer especially must be able to catch the "sequence of motion and fact which made the emotion and which would be as valid in a year or ten years or, with luck and if you stated it purely enough, always. . . ."[22]

Hemingway, then, is a novelist who wanted to, or had to, write about death in a deathless prose. A clumsy but accurate title for his collected works might be "How to Die Correctly in Ten Not Very Easy Lessons." Anyone, the implication is, can live and die sloppily (take the case of Sam Cardinella in Chapter XV, one of those ironic fillers in *In Our Time:* "When they came toward him with the cap to go over his head Sam Cardinella lost control of his sphincter muscle. . . ."; or take the case of Harry in "Kilimanjaro," *i.e.,* his stinking gangrenous death as opposed to his imagined flight). The trick is to die with as much dignity as the pressure of the world will allow. Grace under pressure, purity of line—these are the guiding phrases. They stand for living, dying, and writing; but the living and dying can be combined, because when we are being told how to live better by Hemingway, we are being told how to die better. Death and writing are the two best fixatives; they freeze the material into its final mold.

Through Goya's art Hemingway found part of his own esthetic principle, in the form of pure-lined etchings that employ grays and whites in shadowing out the forms of life and death. Through bull fighting he found the momentary sculptural effect of arrested motion, which is impermanent, and the cohesiveness of tragic

[22] *Ibid.,* pp. 2, 278.

ritual, which is relatively permanent. Subsumed under the general heading of esthetics, however, are two other elements of Hemingway's art that must be accounted for—his own peculiar brand of the objective (perhaps *imagistic*) correlative, and his organic, realistic symbolism.

T. S. Eliot has received full recognition for formally defining "objective correlative" as literary technique in his essay on Hamlet in *The Sacred Wood,* where he states how a set of objects and events associated with an emotion in a given instance can, in turn, work to re-create that emotion for the reader. Hemingway, at least jokingly, has admitted to learning how to use quotations in fiction from Eliot; and it is possible he learned about the objective correlative from him also; at least *The Sacred Wood* was available in Paris in the early 1920's, and Hemingway was closely associated with Ezra Pound, Gertrude Stein, Ford Madox Ford, and others who were aware of what was happening by way of experimentation and theory in writing. Yet in a recent interview (1958) with George Plimpton, Hemingway talked about the objective correlative method as though there might have been a home-grown variety of his own. Plimpton reminded him of a technique that, according to Archibald MacLeish, Hemingway had discovered during his newspaper days; and Hemingway's return comment amounts to an informal definition of the objective correlative:

> What Archie was trying to remember was how I was trying to learn in Chicago in around 1920 and was searching for the unnoticed things that made emotions such as the way an outfielder tossed his glove without looking back to where it fell, the gray colour of Jack Blackburn's skin when he had just come out of stir and other things I noted as a painter sketches. You saw Blackburn's strange colour and the old razor cuts and the way he spun a man before you knew his history. These were the things which moved you before you knew the story.[23]

The "gray colour of Jack Blackburn's skin" is artistically grafted to a certain whiteness of bone in another comment from Hemingway on the use of the objective correlative. In *Death in the Afternoon* he describes lying awake nights trying to piece together what had happened to a certain bull-fighter who had been gored, and then finding the answer to the problem of depiction, as suddenly he gains insight into the scene—"When he stood up, his face *white* and *dirty* and the silk of his breeches opened from waist to knee, it was the *dirtiness* of the rented breeches, the *dirtiness* of his slit underwear and the *clean, clean,* unbearably *clean whiteness*

[23] Plimpton, p. 85.

of the thigh bone that I had seen, and it was that which was important."[24]

Much of Hemingway's art is understandable in reference to the
manner in which he arranges such objects within a flow of action
in an attempt to reproduce the original emotion of the viewer.
To this extent he is not precisely a naturalist—no more, say, than
Stephen Crane, since neither Hemingway nor Crane was interested
simply in showing exactly *how things were,* but *what the feelings
are* in respect to how things were. The selective qualities of these
two writers produce a much more concentrated effect than that of
such broad-gauge naturalists as Zola, Dreiser, Norris, and Farrell.
This concentrative effort accounts for the successful application of
Hemingway's simplified prose, since a style depending largely
upon substantives of a colorless and unobtrusive nature (here
Hemingway takes leave of Crane) has an excellent chance of
moving the object itself—in objectified, typified form—under the
reader's eye. In this sense, the ultimate in Hemingway's art might
be the presentation of a series of objects set within a time-place-
action continuum, to be quickly replaced by the next series, etc.
But then of course there would be missing the dialogue and the
fixative quality of the prose.

Compared to the objective correlative, Hemingway's type of
organic, realistic symbolism is a much more complicated matter—
difficult to deal with for several reasons. The first is that Hemingway would not cooperate: when asked (in 1958) whether he would
admit to symbolism in his work he answered in a manner calculated to chill even his least exegetical admirers: "I suppose there are
symbols since critics keep finding them. If you do not mind I dis-
like talking about them and being questioned about them. It is
hard enough to write books and stories without being asked to
explain as well. Also it deprives the explainers of work. If five or
six explainers can keep going why should I interfere with them?
Read anything I write for the pleasure of reading it. Whatever
else you find will be the measure of what you brought to the reading."[25]

His symbolism is a difficult matter also because of the critical
response to Hemingway's work. At one end of the scale stand
those—like Ray B. West, Richard Chase, and Leslie Fiedler—who
view the Hemingway product, in large part, as a failure of sensibility; they accept Hemingway as an important American writer,
expecially stylistically, but find his work lacking in sophistication,
intellect, and that rich concatenation of imagery, myth, and sym-

[24] *Death in the Afternoon,* p. 20.
[25] Plimpton, p. 76.

bol which has become so critically important.[26] At the other end of the scale stands Carlos Baker, who (although he warns against "off-the-cuff" allegorists; and provides one of the most valuable approaches to Hemingway's symbolism, with the concept of *sabiduria,* as it applies to "knowledge available under the surface of their lives to all responsive human beings") nevertheless, presents a thesis overly intent on establishing Hemingway as a full-fledged symbolist. Like many pioneer works, his full-length study contains a number of weak spots; and E. M. Halliday has poked an inquiring finger into most of them. After asking hard questions of Baker's overall symbolic interpretation of Hemingway, Halliday concludes his argument with this comment: "To see symbolism as the master device of the earlier novels and short stories tends to obscure another and more characteristic type of ambiguity which makes his best work great fiction in the tacit mode. The extent to which the ironic method has packed his fiction with sub-strata of meaning has not yet, I think, been adequately appreciated in published criticism."[27]

Halliday's commentary rings with accuracy and almost sets matters right about the extent and manner of Hemingway's symbolism. He agrees with Baker that Hemingway works toward symbolic effect by quiet repetition of elements that appeal to the reader's unconscious; but at the end of his article Halliday shies off, calling Hemingway a great "realist" rather than anything else, since the "denomination 'symbolist' has meanings in the common language of criticism that are quite inapplicable to him." Something is lost, however, if we make the terms *symbolist* and *realist* mutually exclusive. Much of that "common language of criticism" to which Halliday refers became common through such works as Edmund Wilson's *Axel's Castle*—in whose first chapter symbolism, or Symbolism, is defined as the poetic application of highly personal, esoteric, and sometimes highly artificial signs by such writers as Baudelaire, Mallarmé, and Viele-Griffin. But at the end of this chapter (after thinking of Proust, Joyce, Gide, and Yeats) Wilson is led to make one of the most important literary pronouncements of his career, and one which certainly pertains in the present instance: "The literary history of our time is to a great

---

[26] This is the critical gist of Ray B. West's "Ernest Hemingway: The Failure of Sensibility," *Sewanee Review* (1945), 120–135; see also Leslie Fiedler's "Adolescence and Maturity in the American Novel," *An End to Innocence* (Boston, 1955), pp. 193–196; and Richard Chase's *The American Novel and Its Tradition* (New York, 1957), p. 204.

[27] E. M. Halliday, "Hemingway's Ambiguity: Symbolism and Irony," *American Literature,* XXVIII (March 1956), 14.

extent that of the development of Symbolism and its fusion or
conflict with Naturalism."

It is precisely here that the imagistic path in the snows of
Ernest Hemingway eventually leads—to a consideration of how his
symbolism fuses or conflicts with his naturalism (or *realism,* as
Halliday would have it). And it may be precisely here that his
reputation is to be decided, for it has become apparent that Hemingway is being critically praised and damned on this very point.
In a recent review of *Hemingway and His Critics,* an international
anthology edited by Carlos Baker, Robert Gorham Davis declares
what may not be statistically precise, but is nevertheless indicative:
"Most of the critics included find Hemingway's symbolism and
allegory more interesting than his realism."[28] But they go a fool's
errand, if we are to believe certain other critics who insist on
throwing Hemingway into unflattering comparison with writers
like Faulkner, Joyce, or Kafka. Caroline Gordon, for example,
declares Kafka a much better symbolist than Hemingway and as
much a naturalist—this in spite of the fact that the story Miss
Gordon makes judgment on is Kafka's "The Hunter Gracchus,"
which has in it a corpse that is still somehow alive and a dove the
size of a rooster that speaks German![29]

Obviously Hemingway is not that kind of super-naturalist;
obviously, too, he is not up to the same kind of beautifully tangled
allegorical methods Kafka is most adept at. Nor need the com-
parision be invidious, either way. The standards of expression
imposed on, or implicit in, Hemingway's work differ from those of
Faulkner, Joyce, or Kafka. For one thing, he was never a practi-
tioner of the symbolic or mythic overlay. His images and symbols
are organic, interior, naturalistic; almost always they come out of
the fictional context (like the matador's *coléta,* a symbol of profession and manhood, in "The Undefeated"; or the hyena, vultures, or
locusts, symbols of oncoming death, in "Kilimanjaro"). Hemingway's attitude toward symbolification is partly explained by this
dialogue between two youths in "The Three-Day Blow":

> "Did you read the Forest Lovers?"
> "Yup. That's the one where they go to bed every night with the naked
> sword between them."
> "That's a good book, Wemedge."
> "It's a swell book. What I couldn't ever understand was what good the

[28] *The New York Times Book Review,* May 14, 1961, p. 4.
[29] Caroline Gordon, "Notes on Hemingway and Kafka," *Sewanee Review,* LVII
(Spring 1949), 214–226; for counter-critical statement see Halliday, pp. 4–5.

sword would do. It would have to stay edge up all the time because if
it went over flat you could roll right over it and it wouldn't make any
trouble."

It's a symbol," Bill said.

"Sure," said Nick, "but it isn't practical."

For Hemingway, as for Nick, it is not enough to have a symbol,
no matter how well established by custom; it has to be "practical"
— that is, meet the demands of reality and fictional context. He
never learned to put symbols in, only draw them out. As a result his
symbolism is non-intellectual, non-allusive; it works on the emotions rather than the mind; it is sensuous and suffused, sometimes
hovering between imagery and metaphor. It is not, however,
simple or primitive, but tends to become equivocal and ironic,
sometimes self-deprecating and occasionally self-defeating (as in
Across the River).

In seeking any final definition of Hemingway's symbols and
accounting for the manner in which they occur, we have to see
them as condensations or illuminations or equations of referents
situationally determined and ironically controlled. This is true of
the numerous snows, rains, ices, and mountains which take on
various meanings in reference to life, death, purity, absolution,
dissolution, perfection, love, castration, frigidity, sterility, etc.
And the effect of this realistic and ironic application of image and
symbol stretches from story to story, novel to novel, as is well
illustrated by the works earlier analyzed in this study. A final example of the ironic tension which can be maintained through symbolic interaction between stories is to be found in Hemingway's treatment of "A Clean, Well-Lighted Place" and "The Light of the
World." In the first of these pieces the imagery is, once again,
predominantly a matter of blacks, whites, and grays: out of a
shadowy sketch emerges the man-made electric light, a modern
secular object which offers temporary salvation to an old man who
cannot be saved by the cathedral gloom of religion. *Light* sym-
bolizes salvation, of sorts. But it has to be considered in its equivocal and ironic form, as found in the second of these two titularly
connected stories (placed side by side in collection). What is the
light of the world, in this second sense? It turns out to be the
Elizabethan "lightness" of the prostitutes (two of them peroxide
blondes, perhaps all three), plus the extreme whiteness of a sodo-
mitic cook's hands (cleansed with lemon juice), and the clean body
of white-hope boxer Steve (Stanley?) Ketchell, knock-out victim
of Negro fighter Jack Johnson. What are we to make of these
strangely symbolic personages? If they represent the light or hope

of the world, the answer is, we are indeed no more saved than the old man in the clean, well-lighted café.

What becomes finally apparent about Hemingway's literary quest is that he was intrigued and caught by a certain line of imagery and symbol—as fascinated by the ambiguous whiteness of snow as Melville was by the ambiguous whiteness of the whale. But Melville was a novelist of magnificently full rhetoric, a Symbolist and Allegorist; Hemingway held to a classically simple rhetoric, and was never a symbolist or allegorist, except in the lower case. The result of Hemingway's artistic scrupulosity may be simplification, but it is also intensification, and a system of imagistic and symbolic cross-references that weave his best works into a single texture.

F. I. Carpenter

Hemingway Achieves the Fifth Dimension

In *Green Hills of Africa,* Ernest Hemingway prophesied: "The kind of writing that can be done. How far prose can be carried if anyone is serious enough and has luck. There is a fourth and fifth dimension that can be gotten." Since then many critics have analyzed the symbols and mythical meanings of Hemingway's prose.[1] A few have tried to imagine what he meant by "a fourth and fifth dimension."[2] But most have agreed that the phrase is pretty vague.

"The fourth dimension" clearly has something to do with the concept of time, and with fictional techniques of describing it. Harry Levin has pointed out that Hemingway's style is lacking in the complexity of structure that normally describes "the third dimension," but that it offers a series of images (much like the moving pictures) to convey the impression of time sequence and immediacy. Joseph Warren Beach has suggested that "the fourth dimension" is related to an "esthetic factor" achieved by the hero's recurrent participation in some traditional "ritual or strategy"; while "the fifth dimension" may be an "ethical factor" achieved by his "participation in the moral order of the world." And Malcolm Cowley has also related "the fourth dimension" of time to "the almost continual performance of rites and ceremonies" suggesting the recurrent patterns of human experience, but has called "the fifth dimension" a "mystical or meaningless figure of speech."

---

[1] See especially Carlos Baker, *Hemingway: The Writer as Artist,* Princeton: 1952, and Philip Young, *Ernest Hemingway,* New York: 1952.

[2] Joseph Warren Beach, "How Do You Like It Now, Gentlemen?" *Sewanee Review,* LIX (Spring, 1951), pp. 311–28; Harry Levin, "Observations on the Style of Hemingway," *Kenyon Review,* XIII (Autumn, 1951), pp. 581–609; Malcolm Cowley, *The Portable Hemingway,* New York: 1944, "Introduction."

But is the prophecy of a fifth-dimensional prose "a meaningless figure of speech"? Certainly Hemingway has often attacked the critics for indulging in grandiose abstractions. Perhaps in *Green Hills of Africa,* one of his poorer books, he may have lowered his guard and relaxed his muscles. "The fifth dimension," moreover, has no accepted meaning to modern physicists. But Hemingway's art has always been self-conscious, and in the years of his apprenticeship in Paris he often discussed this art with Gertrude Stein—a trained philosopher, and an admirer of Henri Bergson's theories of the two kinds of "time."[3] Finally, I think, "the fifth dimension" is too strikingly specific a figure of speech to be "meaningless," although it may be "mystical."[4]

Actually, the specific phrase "the fifth dimension" was used in 1931 (*Green Hills of Africa* was published in 1935), by P. D. Ouspensky, who defined it to mean "the perpetual now." Ouspensky, a mystic, was an admirer of Bergson and of William James. Bergson (also an admirer of James) had emphasized the difference between psychological time and physical time. And both these ideas go back to William James's philosophy of "radical empiricism" (that is, of "immediate" or "pure" experience), which Gertrude Stein (a former pupil of James) had adapted for literary purposes. There is strong internal evidence that Hemingway's philosophy and practice both of style and of structure have followed this pattern of philosophic ideas. His literary ideal has been that of "immediate empiricism." And his "fifth-dimensional prose" has attempted to communicate the immediate experience of "the perpetual now."

This mystical idea of a "fifth-dimensional" experience of "the perpetual now" might seem fantastic except that Hemingway first suggested it explicitly, and then practiced it consciously in his best fiction. *For Whom the Bell Tolls* embodies the idea both implicitly, in structure, and explicitly, in the speeches and thoughts of its characters. If this major novel is analyzed with this philosophic idea in mind, the structure and the purpose become unmistakable. The same structure (although less explicitly) informs the two great short stories which preceded this novel: "The Short Happy Life of Francis Macomber" and "The Snows of Kilimanjaro." And the writing of these three major works immediately followed Hem-

---

[3] See Bergson, *Durée et Simultanéité: à propos de la théorie d'Einstein,* Paris: 1922.

[4] I use the term "mystical" in its most general sense, to describe any intense experience or "ecstasy" which results in insight or "illumination." I have defined this kind of mysticism at length in my *Emerson Handbook,* New York: 1953, pp. 113–16.

ingway's prophecy of a "fifth dimension" to be achieved by prose.

Finally, this idea of "the perpetual now," and the philosophy of immediate empiricism which underlies it, suggest an explanation for the sharp alternation of brilliant success and painful failure in Hemingway's fictional career. In its sentimental or isolated form, this idea degenerates into "the cult of sensation,"[5] or of violent experience divorced from the routine of living. In this form it explains the frequent spectacular badness of *To Have and Have Not* and of *Across the River and into the Trees*. But when related to the routine experiences of life, which give the more "sensational" experiences both a frame of reference and a meaning, this philosophy suggests the heights to which human nature can rise in moments of extreme stress. No longer the cult of "sensation," it becomes the ideal of "intensity" or "ecstasy," and produces that telescoping of experience and those flashes of illumination which make the "short" life of Francis Macomber supremely "happy," and the snows of Kilimanjaro blindingly brilliant.

In the 1920s, Albert Einstein's scientific theory of relativity— with its interpretation of "time" as a fourth dimension necessary to the measurement of the space between the stars and within the atoms—spawned a generation of pseudo-scientific speculators who attempted to interpret the meaning of these physical theories for philosophic and literary purposes. The most spectacular (and the least scientific) of these was the Russian-born mystic, P. D. Ouspensky, who published his *Tertium Organum* in 1921, and *A New Model of the Universe* in 1931. Specifically, Ouspensky defined the "fifth dimension" as

> a line of perpetual now. . . . The fifth dimension forms a surface in relation to the line of time. . . . Though we are not aware of it, sensations of the existence of other "times" continually enter our consciousness. . . . The fifth dimension is movement in the circle, repetition, recurrence.[6]

And at considerable length he analyzed and illustrated these pseudo-scientific ideas with reference to James's "moments of consciousness," Bergson's theory of time, and "the Eternal Now of Brahma." I do not mean to imply that Hemingway necessarily read Ouspensky's books, but his conversations with Gertrude Stein and her friends in the twenties might well have included discussion of

---

[5] See R. P. Warren, "Hemingway," *Kenyon Review,* IX (Winter, 1947), pp. 1–28.

[6] *A New Model of the Universe* (first published 1931, rev. ed., New York: 1950), p. 375.

them. Moreover, his specific reference to "a fifth dimension" finds partial explanation here, and Ouspensky's description of "the perpetual now" closely parallels passages in *For Whom the Bell Tolls* (as we shall see later).

With Bergson's theory of the "fourth dimension" of time, we approach firmer ground. Closer to the main stream of philosophic thought, Bergson tried to interpret Einstein's scientific theory of the relativity of time for literary purposes. In 1922 he used recent experiments measuring the speed of light, and proving that light rays are "bent" by the force of gravitation, to illustrate his own already published theories of time. If physical "time" may be distorted by motion in space and by gravitation, the measurement of psychological time may be distorted even more. Bergson had always emphasized that mechanic time could never measure the intensities of the *élan vital* in human experience, and that the human organism distorted "time" through the devices of memory and intuitional thought. Now Einstein's theory of relativity suggested that time was not a final measurement in physics, either. In human consciousness time might be telescoped, and sensation intensified, just as a passenger on a train approaching a warning signal at a road crossing hears the ringing intensified in pitch as he approaches. Again, these ideas find echoes in Hemingway's prose.

But all these ideas are speculative. The matrix from which they spring, and in which their "mysticism" finds relation to reality, is the philosophy of William James—acknowledged as "master" by Ouspensky, Bergson, and Gertrude Stein equally. Approaching philosophy by way of psychology, James had interpreted all religious and artistic experiences as empirical phenomena: he had sought to observe, report, and analyze those intense "moments of consciousness," which men of religion and of art alike have described as the most "real" and important. With James, therefore, "realism" had become psychological, and "empiricism" had expanded to include all "immediate" or subjective as well as "mediate" or objective experience. Studying under James, Gertrude Stein had developed artistic techniques for communicating this "immediate" experience in prose style. Hemingway now carried these techniques further, and incorporated their psychological and philosophic patterns (outlined by James. Bergson, and perhaps Ouspensky) in the structural forms of his fiction.

To trace the development of these philosophic ideas, and to illustrate their application to literature, a book would hardly suffice. But to summarize: A brief, immediate experience, observed realistically, is described first as it occurred "in our time"; the protagonist is intensely moved, but remains confused, so that the meaning of it all seems nothing, or "nada." But this immediate experience recalls individual memories of other, similar experiences, or historic memories of parallel experiences in the history of other nations, or mystical, "racial" memories. And these "mediate" experiences are suggested by "flashbacks," or by conversations, or by the suggestion of recurrent myth or ritual patterns. And these fragmentary remembrances of similar experiences, by relating the individual to other people, places and times, suggest new meanings and forms. Finally this new awareness of the patterns and meanings implicit in the immediate, individual experience intensified it, happened.

For Whom the Bell Tolls is Hemingway's first full-length novel to describe, and partially to achieve, this radical intensification of experience. Both explicitly and implicitly, it seeks to realize the "fifth dimension" of an "eternal now," beyond the usual "fourth dimension" of time. It consciously describes—as well as subconsciously suggests—the telescoping of time involved in this realization of immediate experience. Indeed the very explicit self-consciousness with which it describes this idea constitutes its chief fault. But, although the idea has been suggested before, its formal pattern has never been clarified.

On the surface, the novel describes the tragedy of an American volunteer, fighting for the Loyalists in the Spanish Civil War, who is sent to dynamite a bridge and does so, but is killed as a result. The action takes place in three days and involves a love affair with a Spanish girl named Maria, who has been rescued by the band of Communist guerrillas, after having been raped by the Fascists. This love affair has been criticized as irrelevant and obtrusive, but it actually forms the core of the book. And paradoxically it seems obtrusive *because* it struggles under so heavy a weight of conscious meaning.

The love affair begins immediately (and sensationally) when Maria crawls into the hero's sleeping bag the first night out. She hopes thus to exorcise the memory of the evil that has been done to her. But, even while loving her, the hero remains conscious of the passage of time, asking "'what time is it now?' . . . It was one o'clock. The dial showed bright in the darkness that the robe made."[7] Later when he declares his love for Maria to Pilar, the gypsy mother-confessor, she warns him that "There is not much time." Because the ending is destined to be tragic, the love affair must be brief. But it will be meaningful, later.

[7] *For Whom the Bell Tolls,* New York: 1940, p. 72.

After the second experience of love on the second day, this new meaning is suggested: ". . . and time absolutely still and they were both there, time having stopped and he felt the earth move out and away from under them." Later, thinking of this experience, the hero generalizes:

> . . . Maybe that is my life and instead of it being threescore years and ten it is . . . just threescore hours and ten or twelve rather. . . .
>
> I suppose it is possible to live as full a life in seventy hours as in seventy years; granted that your life has been full up to the time that the seventy hours start and that you have reached a certain age.
>
> . . . So if your life trades its seventy years for seventy hours I have that value now and I am lucky enough to know it. . . . If there is only now, why then now is the thing to praise. . . . Now, *ahora, maintenant, heute.*

This telescoping of time becomes the new "value," and a universal one. Meanwhile, the hero continues to speculate about this tragic and enigmatic wisdom suggested by Pilar, the gypsy:

> . . . She is a damned sight more civilized than you and she knows what time is all about. Yes, he said to himself, I think that we can admit that she has certain notions about the value of time. . . .
>
> Not time, not happiness, not fun, not children, not a house, not a bathroom, not a clean pair of pyjamas, not the morning paper. . . . No, none of that. . . .
>
> So if you love this girl as much as you say you do, you had better love her very hard and make up in intensity what the relation will lack in duration and in continuity.

As explicitly as possible the hero develops these new "notions about the value of time," speculating that the intense experience of a perpetual "now" may equal in value a lifetime of "duration and continuity." "It was a good system of belief," he concluded. "There is nothing else than now. . . . A good life is not measured by any biblical span."

In the ecstatic experience of perfect union with his beloved, time has stood still, and the value of intensity has been substituted for that of duration. From this experience has emerged the philosophy of the eternal now. Meanwhile, as the larger action of the novel approaches its climax, the hero seeks to understand the strange combination of violence and idealism which characterizes the Spanish people.

On the last night, Maria pours out to him the story of her violation. And again he generalizes:

> Those are the flowers of Spanish chivalry. What a people they have been. . . . Spain has always had its own special idol worship within the Church. *Otra Virgen más.* I suppose that was why they had to destroy the virgins of their enemies. . . . This was the only country the reformation never reached. They were paying for the Inquisition now, all right. . . .
>
> Maybe I have had all my life in three days, he thought.

In the hero's mind, "Maria" thus becomes a symbol of the traditional mariolatry of the Spanish Catholic Church, which "the reformation never reached"; and the violence of the Spanish Civil War becomes an intensified version of all modern history since the Reformation, compressed in symbolic time. His love for this modern Maria becomes both a symbolic fulfillment of history and a transcendence of the old "time." In a flash, the immediate experience of the eternal now becomes not only a personal "system of belief," but a philosophy of history illuminating the action of the whole novel.

Shortly after, the third and final experience of love obliterates time ("the hand on the watch moved, unseen now"), the ecstasy is complete ("not why not ever why, only this now"), and this individual experience becomes one with the experience of all mystics: "It is in Greco and in San Juan da la Cruz, of course, and in the others. I am no mystic, but to deny it is as ignorant as though you denied the telephone." And this mystic transcendence of time and of self informs the final chapters of the book, as, after being fatally wounded, the hero comforts Maria: "Thou art me too now. Thou art all there will be of me" (p. 464), and accepts his own death: "He began to accept it and let the hate go out. . . . Once you saw it again as it was to others, once you got rid of your own self, the always ridding of self that you had to do in war. Where there could be no self." Thus finally the experience of "the perpetual now" leads to the mystical experience.

This intensification of experience under the emotional stress of love or war, resulting in an ecstasy transcending the traditional limitations of time and of self, and producing a "system of belief" verging on the mystical, is the subject of *For Whom the Bell Tolls,* both implicitly and explicitly. In a sense it has always been the subject of all Hemingway's fiction. But of course the emphasis has changed over the different periods of his writing, and he has developed this "system of belief" progressively.

Hemingway's early fiction, in general, described the immediate experience, of love or war, with a minimal awareness of meaning, and a minimal experience of ecstasy; therefore the experience seemed largely "sensational," and the meaning "nada." But beginning with "The Short Happy Life of Francis Macomber" and "The Snows of Kilimanjaro," his stories began to achieve ecstasy and to imagine a transcendence of the futility of the past. The sudden illumination of the vision of snow-capped Kilimanjaro prophesied the ecstasies and the transcendence of time in *For Whom the Bell Tolls*. But this novel exaggerated perhaps the author's new consciousness of meaning, and his concern with the "system" of his belief. In *The Old Man and the Sea* the idea became at last incarnated and the mysticism completely naturalized.

But the idea of the intensified experience of the immediate "now" is not simple, nor is its mysticism traditional. Hemingway himself has suggested some of the necessary qualifications: his Robert Jordan "supposed" that the final fulfillment of life in seventy hours was possible, "granted that your life has been full up to the time that the seventy hours start, and that you have reached a certain age." That is, the intensity of experience which transcends time, and achieves a new "value" or "dimension," depends upon an earlier fullness of experience of time and the appreciation of its value. The mysticism of this fifth-dimensional experience implies no denial of the old "values" or "dimensions," but rather a fulfillment beyond them. These heroes do not seek escape from time (as do the hero and heroine of Robert Penn Warren's *World Enough and Time*), nor do they build a "tower beyond tragedy" (like the heroes of Robinson Jeffers), but rather they seek the intensified fulfillment of life within tragedy.

Further, this achievement of a new dimension of experience requires maturity—the hero must have reached "a certain age." Besides having lived a full life in the past, he must have reached a turning point, or crisis of life. So Francis Macomber—a natural aristocrat who has excelled at sports in the past—confronts the final test of courage, fails, but suddenly overcomes his fear and achieves a brief ecstasy of happiness. And the autobiographical hero of Kilimanjaro—who has prospered well enough in love and in literature—sees suddenly the ecstatic vision of supreme success, as he dies.

Finally, the achievement of this new dimension of experience, whether in "prose" or in life, is exceptional—"one must have luck."

So Robert Jordan "had learned that he himself, with another person, could be everything. But inside himself he knew that this was the exception." The new experience requires a fullness of past life, a certain age, and an ecstasy which is mystical in every sense.

A fourth-dimensional sense of time (Cowley and Beach have suggested) is often achieved by a detailed description of the patterns of experience which have crystallized in rituals, ceremonies, traditions, habits of action, codes of behavior. On the level of pure realism, this may be suggested by that loving description of the techniques of any work or sport which is characteristic of all Hemingway's stories.[8] The absence of this workaday realism contributes to the failure of *Across the River,* while the exact techniques of fishing make real the occasional mysticism of *The Old Man and the Sea.* On the level of art, the patterned ritual of the bullfight and the sporting code of the big-game hunter also suggest this sense of repetition in time. While on the level of religion, mythical or symbolic actions, which sometimes seem unreal or irrational, may provide the pattern. The esthetic sense of the perfect fulfillment of some pattern of action in time is the necessary precondition for achievement of the final "magic."

The "fifth-dimensional" intensity of experience beyond time may come, finally, from a profound sense of participation in these traditional patterns of life experience. Beach's description of the fifth dimension as a "sense of participation in the moral order of the world" is suggestive. "You felt an absolute brotherhood with the others who were engaged in it," observed Robert Jordan of his Spanish Civil War. Paradoxically, love and war become supremely "moral," and the intensity of the experience they offer may communicate a mystical ecstasy. If only the sensational and the violent aspects are described, with only a traditional, third-dimensional realism, "nada" results. But these violent sensations have always been the elemental stuff, both of human tragedy and of mystical transcendence. If the red slayer think only of slaying, and if the slain think only of being slain, no fourth or fifth dimension is achieved. But Santiago in *The Old Man and the Sea,* performing realistically the ritual techniques of his trade, goes on to identify the intensity of his own suffering with that of the great fish that he is slaying. And, telling his story, Hemingway has achieved that synthesis of immediate experience and mysticism which, perhaps, is "the fifth dimension."

---

[8] See Joseph Beaver, "'Technique' in Hemingway," *College English* (March, 1953), p. 325.

Daniel Fuchs

Ernest Hemingway, Literary Critic

I

Though the critics have found many things to praise in Hemingway, his mind was seldom one of them. Dwight Macdonald, in a funny if unoriginal essay, seems to express the consensus in saying that there is little evidence of thought in his writing, that for all his sureness of "instinct" as a writer, he strikes one as not particularly intelligent.[1] And Leslie Fiedler points to a pervasive humorlessness, a shortcoming of mind, in him as a writer.[2] If the critics have been sharks to Hemingway's Santiago, it is also a case of man bites shark. Who more proudly flaunted his contempt of them? Who was the first to make megalomania part of the novelist's personal style—as if critical intelligence were exercised only by those who live life all the way from the neck up? Yet Hemingway was a writer whose diction, whose tone, whose very existence as an artist imply a relationship with literary culture no less certain than that of the mythical New York beasts he excoriates.[3] I am not speaking of his characteristic literary ideas, his typical confrontations, his dilemmas and resolutions, the topography of his fictional world, about which much has been said, but of a more purely speculative function in which a particular prose or literary position or artist's reputation is under scrutiny, whether in direct comment or tangential

[1] Dwight Macdonald, "Ernest Hemingway," *Encounter,* XVIII, 116–117 (Jan., 1962).

[2] Leslie Fiedler, "Hemingway in Ketchum," *Partisan Review,* XXIX, 396, 398 (Summer, 1962).

[3] For his most extreme statement on "New York literary reviews," see Hemingway's preface to Elio Vittorini's *In Sicily.* Nowhere in his work is there such a density of, shall we say, humanistic tropes.

remark. Though this is an admittedly bookish approach to Hemingway, it is one he has still to gain by, and the very fact that it can be congenial indicates a kind of resilience to his intelligence that is not often associated with it. He was a critic in spite of himself. What is more, he had a more than tacit commitment to a particular cast of literary mind which in terms of his own preferences constitutes a tradition; this commitment makes clear the extent and quality of his humor.

For all his one-time modernity, for all his appropriation of a unique style, for all his Bohemianism, Hemingway is in a literary tradition as old as the novel itself. If we are looking for illustrious forefathers we may go as far back as *Don Quixote*. Leicester Hemingway, in his biographical reminiscence, recalls the following: "Ernest said there had been some wonderful men in the recent human past. These included Cervantes, Cellini and the Elizabethans."[4] And in *Death in the Afternoon* Hemingway tells us that he has "cared for" Cervantes, one of the very few writers who wrote before the nineteenth century whom he has made a point of complimenting.[5] Another is Fielding. He seems to have known Fielding well and felt the presence of a somehow kindred spirit to the extent that he quotes parts of the preface to *Joseph Andrews* as introductory squibs in his parody of Anderson, *The Torrents of Spring*. More than this, Fielding is the only author on Hemingway's fullest list of "musts" for young writers who wrote before the nineteenth century.[6] Along with the expected works of Stendhal, Flaubert, Tolstoy, we find him singling out *Joseph Andrews* and *Tom Jones* as part of the novel's most distinguished pedigree. His preference for Fielding should not surprise us, since he sees the unheroic hero in the world of his imagining and consistently mistrusts the elevated, the mystical, the glorious, the grand. In attacking Waldo Frank's *Virgin Spain* as "bedside mysticism"[7] he makes a remark which all innovators of realistic fiction would applaud: "All bad writers are in love with the epic."[8] (The comic epic in prose is another thing.) Parody, mistrust of the heroic, Cervantes, Fielding. The point I wish to make in this essay is that Hemingway is in what may be called the novel in burlesque tradition—burlesque conceived in its broadest range of sense, from explicit parody to

[4] Leicester Hemingway, *My Brother, Ernest Hemingway* (Cleveland, 1962), p. 171.
[5] *Death in the Afternoon* (New York, 1932), p. 73.
[6] *Esquire*, IV, 21, 174a, 174b (Oct., 1935).
[7] *Death in the Afternoon*, p. 53.
[8] *Ibid.*, pp. 35–36.

implicit criticism. Hemingway is one of those writers who would not have written so well had others not written so poorly or, as the case may be, so differently, one of those novelists for whom the novel has been, among other things, literary criticism. Flaubert, Joyce, Mark Twain—all of whom he held in the highest regard—are others. All of these gave a new meaning to the word realism.

Ezra Pound once remarked that Hemingway is pre-eminently the wiseguy,[9] and though Delmore Schwartz dismisses this as an extravagance, Pound is here, as he often is, profoundly right about a literary peer. Hemingway's prose is indeed motivated by a comic contempt of standard English in its aspect of respectability, gentility, polite euphemism, though it never forgets it in its aspect of biblical plainness and repetition. Furthermore, as we shall have occasion to see, his wiseguy intransigence is manifest so often in the way he builds a scene, conceives a character, projects a vision, that it, as much as anything else, marks his characteristic style. This is at the heart of his critical sense. When this is understood, Macdonald's remarks, say, about Hemingway's affinity to his "opposites . . . Stendhal and Tolstoi—interesting that he should feel awed by them—who had no style at all, no effects"—will be easily countered. For example, what writer could we associate more with the battle initiations of Fabrice del Dongo and Nickolai Rostov than Hemingway? Hemingway's joke, his *Kunst,* lies in showing that things as they really are are different from what they are like in story books and political speeches, that the writer's duty is to cut away the imaginative deadwood, that realism is so often, in Tolstoy's phrase, "making things strange," that the wiseguy can be the source of an unexpected, bracing wisdom. Hemingway's distinction as a writer is that he considered this insight not only as matter but as manner. Macdonald speaks of him as if his writing were separable from his mind, which may be the reason he finds so little intelligence in him.

Hemingway, in short, like Cervantes, Fielding, Stendhal, Flaubert, Mark Twain, and Joyce, writes what is in this sense an antiliterary literature. Like that of many of the modernists of the twenties, Hemingway's work was at first hardly considered literature at all. Reminiscing about the early Paris days, he considers "all of the stories back in the mail that came in through a slit in the saw mill door, with notes of rejection that would never call

[9] Quoted by Delmore Schwartz in *Ernest Hemingway: The Man and His Work,* ed. John K. M. McCaffery (Cleveland and New York, 1950), p. 114.

them stories, but always anecdotes, sketches, contes, etc."[10] The genteel American response to his work was typified by his parents. His mother (a reader of Walter Scott who named her summer place "Windemere") and father returned *In Our Time* and were "bewildered and shocked" by *The Sun Also Rises*.[11] One need only teach *In Our Time* to observe even now the curious mixture of reverence and confusion in response to it.

Hemingway did not write better prose than that which appears in the *In Our Time* sequence (he has, of course, done worse), and it is this prose which registers as clearly as any his wiseguy stance. "On the Quai at Smyrna," which is an introductory sketch, exhibits a tension between the comfortable, genteel English of the English captain who is narrator and the war experience which it cannot seem to contain. Listening to the dispossessed women, he says, "The strange thing was . . . [how] they screamed at that time." They would be "quieted" by the searchlight: "That always did the trick." The dead ones had to be "cleared off" the pier. One was a "most extraordinary case" — the one whose legs drew stiff. Where English is capable of recording the shock of war it is in a Gulliver-like recording of detail. The euphemism, the detachment of the captain's manner is painfully modified by what he actually sees. But the captain seems to be aware of the inability of his language to express his feelings. Hence his irony in describing the harbor: "There were plenty of nice things floating around in it. That was the only time in my life I got so I dreamed about things." In his nervous matter-of-factness the Englishman sounds like a grown-up Huck Finn. "The Greeks were nice chaps too. When they evacuated they had all their baggage animals they couldn't take with them so they just broke their forelegs and dumped them into the shallow water. . . . It was all a pleasant business. My word yes a most pleasant business." The final turn of the screw is that his casual, genteel manner explodes in his face as his intended irony becomes indistinguishable from it.

This opening sketch about the Greco-Turkish war is connected to the final vignette in which Hemingway, or a surrogate, is interviewing the Greek king. A tension exists between the grim realities of revolutionary politics and the inanities of genteel conversation. Perhaps the best example of this deflationary technique is the Chapter IV vignette.[12]

[10] *Green Hills of Africa* (New York, 1935), p. 70.

[11] *My Brother, Ernest Hemingway,* p. 100.

[12] *The Short Stories of Ernest Hemingway* (New York, 1953), pp. 87–88, 113.

> It was a frightfully hot day. We'd jammed an absolutely perfect barricade across the bridge. It was simply priceless. A big old wrought-iron grating from the front of a house. Too heavy to lift and you could shoot through it and they would have to climb over it. It was absolutely topping. They tried to get over it, and we potted them from forty yards. They rushed it, and officers came out alone and worked on it. It was an absolutely perfect obstacle. Their officers were very fine. We were frightfully put out when we heard the flank had gone, and we had to fall back.

Here again Hemingway observes the inadequacies of a language not equipped to deal with the destructive realities, an Englished language echoing from afar the terms of hunting and country festivities. Though the language is English, the way it is scrutinized is American. That the barricade is "perfect . . . simply priceless . . . absolutely topping" does not blend well with the murderous activity in which the English are both agents and victims. Then, too, being "frightfully put out" when the flank goes is something of a different order from a frightfully hot day. The docility of the language intensifies the panic, all of which is to the writer's credit. It may well be, as Carlos Baker informs us, that Hemingway is here imitating the speech of his friend Captain E. E. Dorman-Smith. But the use he is making of it has little relevance to friendship.

The most sustained piece Hemingway has done in this vein is the rarely noticed story, "A Natural History of the Dead." In conception a small *tour de force,* it is a montage of two violently dissonant prose styles: the first we are to take as standard English; the second as vintage Hemingway. The standard English style is not identifiable as the style of any of the four stooges named—W. H. Hudson, Gilbert White, Bishop Stanley, and Mungo Park: rather it is a mock-gentleman style which attempts to give us the essence of the English clubman's adventure story. The wiseguy irony implicit is that naturalistic adventure should be rendered so unadventurously, so prissily, as if Africa were an extension of the club. Mungo Park is quoted in pastiche; the stiff-upper-lip confidence of his prose is almost indistinguishable from Hemingway's parody.

> When that persevering traveller, Mungo Park, was at one period of his course fainting in the vast wilderness of an African desert, naked and alone, considering his days as numbered and nothing appearing to remain for him to do but to lie down and die, a small moss-flower of extraordinary beauty caught his eye.

"Though the whole plant," says he, "was no larger than one of my fingers, I could not contemplate the delicate confirmation [*sic*] of its roots, leaves and capsules without admiration. Can that Being who planted, watered and brought to perfection, in this obscure part of the world, a thing which appears of so small importance, look with unconcern upon the situation and suffering of creatures formed after his own image? Surely not. Reflections like these would not allow me to despair; I started up and, disregarding both hunger and fatigue, travelled forward, assured that relief was at hand; and I was not disappointed."[13]

In Hemingway's story Park is always "that persevering traveller" and he perseveres because, like Bishop Stanley, he knows that the study of Natural History is linked with an increase in faith, in "the protecting eye of that Providence." Park, who starts out (attempting to ascertain the course of the Niger) in a blue coat with yellow buttons and ends up two and a half years later naked, drinking at a trough between two cows, is more subject to despair than Hemingway will allow. Parody, however, is not known for its qualities of fairness. There is, in fact, a somewhat unwarranted calm about the Scot's prose and manner. It contrasts sharply with the hysteria, the *nada,* which Hemingway chillingly conveys in the second half of the story (after some funny transitions). Nor is Park's prose designed to record things memorably; an elephant is a "powerful and docile creature," a native a "poor untutored slave."

War is what Hemingway is talking about in the story. When he writes, "Let us therefore see what inspiration we may derive from the dead," he is attempting a *reductio* of the providential: "One wonders what that persevering traveller, Mungo Park, would have seen on a battlefield in hot weather to restore his confidence . . . and have any such thoughts as Mungo Park about those formed in His own image." Associating the providential and the idea of an ennobling death weighted with significance with the so-called Humanist literary movement, which in a mock-footnote he calls "an extinct phenomenon," Hemingway flaunts his first-hand experience of war like so many medals. If Hemingway's accusation that the Humanists were "dead in their youth of choice" is hysterical (it has its ironic point, e.g., Irving Babbitt arriving at his willed, fixed position in his twenties), few would dispute his feeling that the violence at the center of contemporary experience is one of the things that

[13] *Ibid.,* pp. 440–441.

make the Humanist categories seem inadequate. Moreover, the entire piece can be seen in terms of the old realistic priority placed on actuality.

The last section of the piece, all dialogue, emerges as the last refinement in actually being there. In this dialogue the writer records not only the disintegration of abstraction but of language as well. It need hardly be said that the negation expressed in the story does not leave the reader with a sense of all problems solved. What Hemingway succeeded in doing is making his reader more sharply aware of a dubious prose and the too comfortable assumptions supporting it. He has referred to this brutal story as being "written in popular style and . . . designed to be the Whittier's *Snow Bound* of our time." No "angels near at hand" in this frozen cave, no "harmless novel" this, but rather the mind of the writer engaged in the typical modernist stripping away of empty forms.

Probably the most famous passage in Hemingway does precisely this as it at the same time reminds us that this stripping down can be the underside of the coherence one may achieve in the face of its nihilistic potential. Frederic Henry tells us that abstract words like glory, honor, and courage seemed obscene beside the concrete names of villages. Hemingway's work can be seen as an attempt to redefine the actuality these abstractions might have. Pound could easily perceive the satiric thrust which this task inevitably entailed. He had written to Harriet Monroe that good writing needs ideas derived from seeing life in arrangement, the design in life as it exists, not the trying to see life according to an idea.[14] Pound taught his friends to go in fear of abstraction. Polite English became a victim. One of the characteristics of the twenties is that it gave rise to a number of highly stylized literary languages, testimony to the belief that the language, the civilization, needed reappraisal. The assumption that any writer uses English as if he were inventing it is much more relevant to the production of that era than it is to that of our own day. It is part of the orthodoxy of modernism.

---

[14] From a letter of Ezra Pound to Harriet Monroe, in the Harriet Monroe collection in the University of Chicago Library, dated Dec. 15, 1915. Paraphrased with permission of the University of Chicago Library.

II

Hemingway's disenchantment with polite English is general-ized into a pervasive Anglophobia. Often this is fairly explicit, as in Frederic Henry's conversation with Count Greffi.

"Oh, but when you are tired it will be easier for you to talk English."

"American."

"Yes. American. You will please talk American. It is a delight-ful language."[15]

This distinction between American and English is something which Hemingway felt deeply, if hyperbolically. It is, of course, more than a difference in diction and syntax. His very name—Hemingway—was to his wry sense of things too right-sounding, too English; he liked to be called Hemingstein and would sometimes sign his name in letters with even greater comic distortion. For Hemingway "English" often serves as a shorthand for the story-book ending, the providential, the public display, the political rhetoric, the disguise of privileged class, the pseudo-chivalric manner, the exacerbating euphemism of gentility. Occasionally the Hemingway hero will fall into it to his embarrassment as when Frederic Henry is told by Catherine that her fiancé was killed in the battle of the Somme. "It was a ghastly show," he says. "Were you there?" she asks. "No," he replies.[16] In *The Sun Also Rises* a Mrs. Braddocks introduces Robert Prentiss, a rising new novelist from New York by way of Chicago who had, Jake Barnes tells us, "some sort of an English accent." Jake's disgust is immediately evident. Prentiss asks Jake if he finds "Paris amusing?" and Jake is obviously angered. "Oh, how charmingly you get angry. I wish I had that faculty," says Prentiss, adding to Jake's animal repug-nance of him. When Brett tries to brighten his mood he tells her that it has been a "priceless" evening. Brett herself is called Lady Brett when Jake holds her in contempt, when he considers her Englishness: "Brett had a title too. Lady Ashley. To Hell with Brett. To Hell with you, Lady Ashley."[17] And in *The Torrents of Spring,* we are given to believe that it is characteristically English to grace hastily the distinguished new Englishman, the dying Henry

[15] *A Farewell to Arms* (New York, 1929), p. 269.

[16] *Ibid.,* pp. 18–19.

[17] *The Sun Also Rises* (New York, 1926), pp. 21, 30.

James, with the Order of Merit.[18] Similarly, the English tourist is
the most removed for Hemingway, the most unreal. Arriving at
the festival in Pamplona is a "sight-seeing car . . . with twenty-five
Englishwomen in it. They sat in the big, white car and looked
through their glasses at the fiesta. . . . The fiesta absorbed even
the Biarritz English so that you did not see them unless you passed
close to a table." Of course, they are absurd at the bullfight: "The
Biarritz crowd did not like it. They thought Romero was afraid."[19]

Some of Hemingway's best friends are English—or some of
his most amiable characters: Harris in *The Sun Also Rises,* for one
("Take Harris. Still Harris was not of the upper classes," Jake
notes). (Catherine Barkley is Scottish, not English. When asked by
Rinaldi if she loved England, she replies: "Not too well. I'm Scotch,
you see.") It is the English in their aspect of decadent aristocracy
that consistently elicit Hemingway's deflationary wit. "When you
were with the English," Jake says, "you got into the habit of using
English expression in your thinking. The English spoken language
—the upper classes, anyway—must have fewer words than the
Eskimo."[20] And the Hemingway hero must be some sort of expert
on languages with few words. Nor is this aggression typical of only
the younger Hemingway. No Hemingway hero is more contemp-
tuous of the English than Colonel Cantwell of *Across the River
and Into the Trees:* "'My lady has called twice,' the concierge said
in English. Or whatever that language should be called we all
speak, the Colonel thought. Leave it at English. That is about what
they have left. They should be allowed to keep the name of the
language." His young lady friend wants to learn "American." The
Colonel's anti-English feelings are perhaps even more intense in
his account of Montgomery: "I have seen him come into an hotel
and change from his proper uniform into a crowd-catching kit to
go out in the evening to animate the populace . . . he is a British
General. Whatever that means." Cantwell adds to this description
of "Field Marshal Bernard Law Montgomery" the information that
he knew he was not great.[21]

It is as if English were the source of most civilized evasions
and distortions, a severe case, a monolithic instance of what Lawrence calls mental consciousness. Hemingway, too—in a parallel
which does not imply an identity—encountered the dominant
culture with disgust and aggression, countering respectability with

[18] *The Hemingway Reader* (New York, 1953), p. 51.
[19] *Op. cit.,* pp. 205, 217.
[20] *Ibid.,* p. 149.
[21] *Across the River and Into the Trees* (New York, 1951), pp. 195, 206, 134.

an aesthetic primitivism, an intellectual Bohemianism. There is a balance in his work between primitivism and culture, between the physical ordeal, the victory of the code character and the brooding though anti-rational intelligence of the hero. He is, in Richard Chase's phrase, a highbrow-lowbrow,[22] or, to put it another way, he is a redskin half-paleface. He portrays defiance and grace in terms which are more than physical, making a raid upon a faltering cultural style. His Anglophobia is not to be strictly equated with a hatred of all things English so much as it is to be understood as a symbol of the failure of a gentility which results in a turning from life.

What is most inimical to Hemingway is the tradition of American literature he identifies as English. He maintains that "Emerson, Hawthorne, Whittier and Company wrote like exiled English colonials from an England of which they were never a part to a newer England that they were making. Very good men with small, dried and excellent wisdom of Unitarians; men of letters; Quakers with a sense of humor." What is perhaps most valuable in Hemingway's judgment is the clarity of his rejection in relation to his own writing. "All these men were gentlemen or wished to be. They were all very respectable. They did not use the words that people always have used in speech, the words that survive in language. Nor would you gather they had bodies. They had minds, yes. Nice, dry, clean minds."[23] If there is a broad truth in Hemingway's remarks it is of the kind that resides in John Jay Chapman's hyperbolic remark that the one thing a man in the future would not be able to know from our mid-nineteenth century writers (with Hawthorne an obvious exception here too) is that there were two sexes in America. But even the broad truth should not have completely blinded him to the fact that Emerson, albeit in a very different way, was very much engaged in the transformation of cultural values, in defining what was new world and how the new world was superior to the old. Extravagant as Hemingway's judgment may seem to be, it is more or less the going judgment of the polite, occasional, literary, picturesque, Europe-imitating schoolroom poets.

[22] *The Democratic Vista* (New York, 1958), p. 52.

[23] *Green Hills of Africa,* p. 21. Longfellow, too, is fair game: "Someone with English blood has written, 'Life is real, life is earnest, and the grave is not its goal.' And where did they bury him? And what became of the reality of his earnestness?" The apparent objection is to Longfellow's abstract, moralizing quality. Yet the shrill, juvenile quality of the nihilism here expressed makes one think of Longfellow's virtues.

III

Hemingway's criticism comprehends, then, not only a renovation of language but in many cases an involvement with and judgment of other writers. *The Torrents of Spring,* the spirited but slight parody of Anderson in the role of victim of abstraction, almost succeeds in being as funny as *Dark Laughter* often is; it is a minor instance, more important as rehearsal than performance. Hemingway's confrontation of other writers was not merely in the vein of parody nor merely a presence in his minor work. The power of *A Farewell to Arms* is the power of negation, a negation which can be understood as his expression of ideas and evaluation of literary reputations that were very much in the air in the twenties. Carlos Baker mentions Hardy in connection with this novel; an explicit connection can be drawn. The sense of an indifferent cosmos, or even a cruel President of the Immortals underlies the work. The grim confusion of tragedy and farce is also Hardyesque. But Hemingway delineates this confusion in a burlesque dimension. He presents the brutal war as a series of jokes—it never happened this way in the books (except those of Stendhal, Tolstoy, Crane). Frederic Henry is no hero, not even a soldier, but an ambulance driver. And even in this capacity it does not matter whether he supervises the removal of the sick or not. The transference worked better when he was not there. Hurt in battle, he is "blown up while . . . eating cheese." Even if he had had notions of military glory he tells us that his gun jumped so sharply that there was no question of hitting anything. The Italian army itself is disorganized and disenchanted and appears like something out of a comic opera. The soldiers' helmets are not uniform; most of them are too big and come down almost over the ears of the men who wear them. The one "legitimate hero," Moretti, "bored everyone he met with his stories." The Italians fire on themselves. Frederic Henry is suspected of being a German in Italian uniform—the only alternative is the separate peace, the way of the anti-hero. And there is "Oh love, let us be true." But this is a Hardy-cum-Hemingway universe. The ill-omen rain, Catherine's fatalistic feeling about it, the sad, haunting folk refrain (O, western wind), the irrational fear justified by the indifference of the universe, the miscast woman made for a good providence—all these bring Henry to a Hardyesque explanation with a Hemingway twist: "If people bring so much courage to this world the world has to kill them to break them, so of course it kills them. The world breaks everyone and afterward many are strong at the broken places. But those that will not break it kills. It kills the very good and the very gentle and the very brave impartially." Or again, Henry on a modest version of the President of the Immortals: "They threw you in and told you the rules and the first time they caught you off base they killed you."[24]

If Hemingway's nihilism at this point seems lyrical at best or juvenile at worst, it gains in stature by comparison. Henry himself makes the judgments for us in his conversation with Count Greffi as the subject turns to war books. Greffi speaks first:

> "There is 'Le Feu' by a Frenchman, Barbusse. There is 'Mr. Britling Sees Through It [*sic*].'"
> "No, he doesn't."
> "What?"
> "He doesn't see through it. Those books were at the hospital."
> "Then you have been reading?"
> "Yes, but nothing any good."
> "I thought 'Mr. Britling' a very good study of the English middle-class soul."
> "I don't know about the soul."[25]

In the introduction to *Men at War* Hemingway adds to this: "The only good war book to come out during the last war was 'Under Fire' by Henri Barbusse. He was the first one to show us, the boys who went from school or college to the last war, that you could protest in anything besides poetry, the gigantic useless slaughter in generalship that characterized the Allied conduct of the war from 1915 to 1917 . . . when you came to read it over to try to take something permanent and representative from it the book did not stand up. Its greatest quality was his courage in writing the book when he did. They had learned to tell the truth without screaming."[26]

Since both *Under Fire* and *Mr. Britling Sees It Through* ran through several printings in a short time in the United States, Frederic Henry was alluding to well-known books. Barbusse's sensational tone, his egalitarian grievances, his operatic manner, his pacifist editorializing—all give us something of the war that Hemingway does not. But in point of fable, answerable style, sustained psychological portraiture, and accuracy of observation, Hemingway has mastered a subject in part from noticing the short-comings of Barbusse.

He thinks more kindly of him, however, than of H. G. Wells. Britling, an exemplary Britisher, a man of letters who inhabits the

[24] *A Farewell to Arms,* pp. 259, 338.

[25] *Ibid.,* p. 270.

[26] *Men at War,* ed. Ernest Hemingway (New York, 1942), p. 9.

England of "Old John Bull," who considers the backstreets of London "an excrescence," and who believes that "one does not love women, one loves children," is of the genteel, complacent, mental sort that Hemingway likes to abuse. Britling, who despite ominous signs cannot imagine a world war, thinks of the Sarajevo murders as "something out of 'The Prisoner of Zenda.'" The war does break out, and Britling, responding to the narrator's call for a disciplined and clarified will, becomes a special constable. He rationalizes the war as the way the world reconstructs itself and the length of it by the notion that too brief a struggle might lead to a squabble for plunder. The protracted war brings nothing but the death of Mr. Britling's son, his subsequent breakdown, and, finally, his recovery with a wish for a world-federal-republic. If God means anything, thinks Britling, he means tenderness. Wells's novel suggests more than it dramatizes, and its appeal was largely a matter of timeliness. We are given a picture of complacency shattered. Some of the actuality of war is conveyed through the letters of Britling's son. Britling does, in Wells's view, see it through. Henry's point seems to be that he literally did not see much of it at all, or did only from the grandstands. And if Britling's hopeful internationalism and grasping at deity are illustrative of his middle-class soul, these are, for Henry, pale abstractions compared to the experience he has lived through. Henry's mistrust of abstraction, including the middle-class soul, obviously does not blind us to the fact that Britling's ideas are indeed alternatives. The literary point, however, is that in the novel they are almost offhand suggestions. Hemingway is typically associating writing well with telling the truth, the kind of truth *A Farewell to Arms* reveals.

Neither of these novels is important enough to focus Hemingway's main ideas very well. It would take his grappling with writers of greater moment to him than Barbusse and Wells for him to get at the center of his literary position. We have already encountered one of them.

IV

In 1925, Carl Van Doren, writing in the *Century Magazine,* spoke of "two men who have lately divided between them the honors of literary eminence" in England and France: Thomas Hardy and Anatole France.[27] How much of these then giant figures had Hemingway read? There is a juvenilia sketch done in the

[27] *Century Magazine,* CX, 419 (Jan. 25, 1925).

style of France called "A Divine Gesture,"[28] in which God, as much a tyrant as France's Ialdabaoth, convinces his wormlike followers that they must not squirm in dissent. The mingling of the mundane and the theological, the satire of religion with anti-Catholic emphasis, the non-representational quality of a whimsical idea-narrative indicate that Hemingway knew about *The Revolt of the Angels* even if he had not read it.

There is explicit mention of Anatole France and Hardy in *The Sun Also Rises*. Frances, Cohn's impatient mistress, is angry with him:

> "You're thirty-four. Still, I suppose that is young for a great writer. Look at Hardy. Look at Anatole France. He died just a little while ago. Robert doesn't think he's any good though. Some of his French friends told him."[29]

Again the allusion to acknowledged greatness, this time with a difference. From the vantage point of the extreme right, the extreme left, and surrealism, new French writers pointed to Anatole France's vulnerability. For the Americans in Paris, the culture hero whose aesthetic would be the most serious indictment of France was Flaubert. Hemingway has said that he was "the one that we believed in, loved without criticism."[30] His control, his clarity, his rage, his irony—all of these were instructive to the advance-guard expatriates who were indifferent to the loosely strung idea-narratives, the insistent abstraction of the politically-minded later France.

There is a good deal of pastiche in *The Sun Also Rises,* with burlesque references to Mencken and Brooks among the most transparent.[31] There is, moreover, another allusion to Anatole France which is now somewhat obscure but particularly instructive. Bill Gorton tells Jake about "irony and pity"—"They're mad about it in New York"—words which were sacred to Anatole

[28] *Double Dealer,* III, 267–268 (May, 1922).

[29] *Op. cit.,* pp. 50–51.

[30] *Green Hills of Africa,* p. 71.

[31] See pp. 43, 115. Also worth noting is Jake's mention of A. E. W. Mason in that it expresses the old realistic ridicule of the marvelous: "I was reading a wonderful story about a man who had frozen in the Alps and then fallen into a glacier and disappeared, and his bride was going to wait twenty-five years exactly for his body to come out on the moraine, while her true love waited too" (p. 120). Jake also reads from Turgenieff's "A Sportsman's Sketches," which, in its unobtrusive craftsmanship, clarifies and makes sober: "I had read it before but it seemed quite new. The country became quite clear and the feeling of pressure in my head seemed to loosen" (p. 147).

France. Bill and Jake are in Burguete for fishing and Jake is digging for the worms. Bill, thinking of Anatole France, fancies Jake a capitalist type:

> "I saw you out of the window," he said. "Didn't want to interrupt you. What were you doing? Burying your money?"
>
> "You lazy bum!"
>
> "Been working for the common good? Splendid. I want you to do that every morning. . . ."
>
> "Work for the good of all." Bill stepped into his underclothes. "Show irony and pity."
>
> I started out of the room with the tackle bag, the nets, and the rod case. . . .
>
> "Aren't you going to show a little irony and pity?"
>
> I thumbed my nose.
>
> "That's not irony."
>
> As I went downstairs I heard Bill singing, "Irony and Pity. When you're feeling . . . Oh, Give them Irony and Give them Pity. Oh, give them Irony. When they're feeling . . . Just a little irony. Just a little pity. . ." He kept on singing until he came downstairs. The tune was: "The Bells are Ringing for Me and My Gal." I was reading a week-old Spanish paper.
>
> "What's all this irony and pity?"
>
> "What? Don't you know about Irony and Pity?"
>
> "No. Who got it up?"
>
> "Everybody. They're mad about it in New York. It's just like the Fratellinis used to be."[32]

The passage spoofs a well-known Anatolian phrase, the source of which would have been much more familiar to literary men of the twenties than it is to us today. It is from the important prose ramble, *The Garden of Epicurus.*

> The more I think over human life the more I am persuaded we ought to choose Irony and Pity for its assessors and judges, as the Egyptians called upon the goddess Isis and the goddess Nephtys on behalf of their dead. Irony and Pity are both of good counsel; the first with her smiles makes life agreeable; the other sanctifies it with her tears. The Irony I invoke is no cruel deity. She mocks neither love nor beauty. She is gentle and kindly disposed. Her mirth disarms anger and it is she who teaches us to laugh at rogues and fools, whom but for her we might be so weak as to hate.[33]

---

[32] *Ibid.,* pp. 113–114. The Fratellinis are the continental circus act. For Mencken and Brooks, see pp. 43, 115.

[33] *The Garden of Epicurus,* trans. Alfred Allison (New York, 1923), p. 112.

Any discussion of France's irony is complicated by the fact that there are, generally speaking, three phases of it. The irony of *The Crime of Sylvester Bonnard,* an early work, is indeed indulgent and smiling. In *The Garden of Epicurus,* however, as in the contemporaneous *At the Sign of the Reine Pédauque,* the indulgence is more willed than felt. What is genuinely present is a disarmingly playful nihilism bordering on despair. Though there is still a verbal, or somewhat more than verbal, balancing of irony and pity in *The Garden of Epicurus,* by the time France writes the works which now seem his best or at least most popular, *Penguin Island* and *The Revolt of the Angels,* irony stands pretty much alone, stripped of indulgence. It is a bitter irony, the logical extension of the nihilism of *The Garden of Epicurus.* It is hardly likely, then, that "irony and pity" would be understood by literary men in the twenties in its earlier, gentle incarnation. *The Garden of Epicurus* must have been considered in the same context as the later works, a temptation to a despair it was only too easy to feel. Bill Gorton initiates the spoof and he is not only a good friend or even alter ego, but a symbol of Jake's health.

If irony and pity were the rage in New York, or anything resembling it, Hardy, too, most explicitly in *The Dynasts,* would be a reason why. Though Hemingway would never dream of a spirit world, even as an artistic device, the Spirit of the Pities and the Spirits Ironic express a sense of life that paralleled and lent imaginative impetus to post-war themes. As we have seen, *A Farewell to Arms* is an expression of this world veiw. What does relate Hemingway to writers so very different from him as France and Hardy is the pose of the Ecclesiast. Solomon was an old man when he expressed the dim, retrospective view (France and Hardy were always old), but this did not inhibit the young American who, it is clear, had just cause for a pessimistic view. The discrepancy between venerable wisdom and eternal youth is one that would become telling when Hemingway would get only chronologically older.

Irony *is* an important element in Hemingway's fiction; and pity, too, is a subject for his defining. The irony may be the old irony of fate that we get in Catherine's death or Jake's wound or the sharks that plague Santiago. But more characteristic is irony as a matter of tone, as something controlled by Hemingway. That is, the spectatorial irony of France and Hardy, passive with some aggression on the one hand, cruel with some remission on the other, arises out of a sense of loss, a meaninglessness, which Hemingway and his surrogate heroes must do something about to survive. The older fatalism is replaced by stoicism; despite the threat of disintegration, the hero controls. To be sure, the hero is not a consummate expression of the mores and dominant conventions of his society; he finds his integrity in the face of them. But where the irony of Hardy and Anatole France issued into the absurd, the irony of Hemingway is, more characteristically, a sober naming of the ridiculous. The first implies loss, the second a minimal gain. The first is universal in tendency, the second is more expressive of particular men at a particular historical moment. If Jake lacks much conviction, and the worst are full of passionate intensity, the difference between Jake and a character like Krebs, in "Soldiers Home," should be underscored. Jake's negation is selective (though sometimes provincial), a fact which itself implies a vantage point of stabilizing intelligence. Jake is, certainly, an observer; but he is also an actor in a novel whose lessons of morality and style are by now so clear that it emerges as Ernest Hemingway's Morality Play. As an observer, Jake is collaterally related to the straight-man voyagers of eighteenth-century fiction who indirectly expressed the irony of the author. The things they so factually observe! This, of course, is part of the central technical inspiration in *Huckleberry Finn;* as everyone knows, Hemingway owes much to Mark Twain's peculiarly American expression of it (the sensitive, responsible though apparently amoral initiate, the leaving of society, the violence giving over to bad dreams, the mistrust of abstraction, the deflation of the chivalric, the vernacular voice, the lonely equilibrium of self—though Jake is aware of any ironies and not mainly the agent for their indirect expression). It is also related to Flaubert's exemplary irony, which is at base nothing more than his being painfully, mockingly present in a world whose most common occurrences have their own kind of incredibility. The most common meaning the word now possesses in relation to literature is the one which originates in the venerable split between the writer and a society he knows only too well. The code characters notwithstanding, the real hero in Hemingway is his prose and those characters who are a surrogate for the disillusioned irony it expresses. His concept of the hero, accordingly, is one of his burlesque elements. Jake, for example, is not a great lover or a formidable fighter or a thinker who prospers in the rational order derived from a contemplation of disorder. His hero is the private, passive, ultimately modest man, a hero of abnegation, the very precariousness of whose selfhood qualifies him for minimal saintliness, for disinterested action. Yet, if the hero does not win, neither does he lose. If one may pursue the figure, he holds life to a draw, with, among others of a very different stamp, the almost feminine virtues of sensitivity, sympathy, intuition (he is sometimes afraid of the dark and even cries!). Hemingway's criticism of language, then, is also a criticism of personal style, just as it is a criticism of cultural assumptions. His characteristic irony, like that of the novelists in burlesque already named, involves a persistent attitude toward culture, toward books. This is nowhere more apparent than in *The Sun Also Rises.*

At Princeton Robert Cohn "read too much"; in Hemingway's world this is analogous to drinking too much. Cohn lives in a fantasy world.

> He had been reading W. H. Hudson. That sounds like an innocent occupation, but Cohn had read and reread "The Purple Land." "The Purple Land" is a very sinister book if read too late in life. It recounts splendid imaginary amorous adventures of a perfect English gentleman in an intensely romantic land, the scenery of which is very well described. For a man to take it at thirty-four as a guide-book to what life holds is about as safe as it would be for a man of the same age to enter Wall Street direct from a French convent, equipped with a complete set of the more practical Alger books. Cohn, I believe, took "The Purple Land" as literally as though it had been an R. G. Dun report. You understand me, he made some reservations, but on the whole the book to him was sound.[34]

(Cohn's suggestion that he and Jake go off to South America together shows that he had not grasped Hudson's "loner" psychology very well.) If Hardy and Anatole France were a too apparent temptation to despair, W. H. Hudson represented a rainbow evasion of difficult considerations. Should it seem that Jake has too easy game in ridiculing *The Purple Land,* it is to be remembered that Hudson was considered one of the best writers of English prose by no less a judge than Ford Madox Ford.[35] First published in 1885, it was popular enough to be issued in The Modern Library in 1916. This does not prevent one from sharing Jake's opinion of the book. Richard Lamb's tendency to treat women as part of the local color, his wide-eyed primitivism, his political myopia, would support Jake's ironic view. And if Jake is not joking in saying that the scenery is very well described, perhaps he should be: "great plains smiling with everlasting spring; ancient woods; swift beautiful rivers; ranges of blue hills stretching away to the dim horizon. And beyond those fair slopes, how many leagues of pleasant wilderness are sleeping in the sunshine, where the wild flowers

[34] *Op. cit.,* p. 9.
[35] Hemingway includes *Far Away and Long Ago* in his list of exemplary prose works in *Esquire* for October, 1935.

waste their sweetness and no plough turns the fruitful soil."[36]

Hudson's sentimentality, his too easy preference for the inanimate to the human, are symptomatic of the lack of personal responsibility that marks his narrator's debonair adventures. Cohn would be attracted. Jake, one of Hemingway's moral scorekeepers, would not be. Cohn is more of a throwback to the chivalric hero than is the flighty Richard Lamb. When we are almost ready to prefer Cohn's idealized preferences to the broken relationships of everyone else, we need only recall that Cohn is usually wrong in his judgments of others. "I don't believe she could marry anybody she didn't like," he says of Brett. "She's done it twice," Jake answers. Cohn is "ready to do battle for his lady love." Because "he was so sure that Brett loved him. He was going to stay, and true love would conquer all."[37] Part of Cohn's sentimentality is that he can love a woman only in an "affair." Brett is ultimately unattainable, hence desirable. In this sense she is a lost generation Dulcinea, nowhere nearly as perfect as Cohn imagines her to be. Cohn may be seen as a mean, distant relative of Don Quixote; his windmills are ladies, his giants the romanticizing of them. There must be a way other than schoolboy chivalry to dispel the cosmic ironies.

Though the ironies have excluded Jake from the final consummation, they cannot entirely reduce him. His decency remains intact. Though he has suffered a temporary collapse due to Brett's receptivity to all comers, the consequences of this receptivity are not something he could have entirely foreseen. He does what he can to keep Romero from her. The last line of the book—"Isn't it pretty to think so?"—is a sign of Jake's sanity as well as his irony; it names Brett as another who, although she gave up Romero, lives essentially in fantasy. Despite the gloom of much of the book, a good part of it is pervaded by high spirits stemming from the peace of nature and the self-possession of those who have a clear object of ridicule. It should come as no great surprise that Hemingway regarded the book "as in part a humorous one";[38] or that he regarded the lost generation tag as splendid bombast.

Burlesque novelists in the past have often had more to sustain them—a return to happy normalcy, a love for the thing burlesqued. Hemingway has only an attenuated connection with this kind of affirmation; when it is made it is made most typically through the code characters who, in effect, ritualistically overcome a physical

[36] *The Purple Land* (New York, 1916), p. 12.

[37] *Op. cit.,* pp. 178, 199.

[38] Charles Fenton, *The Apprenticeship of Ernest Hemingway* (New York, 1954), p. 203.

crisis analogous to the psychological one that confronts the hero. They overcome the ironies; they are not merely marionettes; their pain has meaning; they help to redefine glory, honor, courage. Hemingway's art is in this way confessional, yet the use of this adjective makes us hasten to add that he has less to say about the meaning of mental suffering. It is this, not the question of whether he had an intelligent encounter with culture, that renders him vulnerable. Hemingway *has* run Huck Finn through life, or part of life; he has stopped short of a maturity that would put him in the same ring with the greatest novelists—as he himself admits in his deferential remarks about Tolstoy. If Hemingway now reads, at times, too much like a classic writer of the twenties, if the artifice of understatement is once again giving over to a more open *cri de coeur,* if it is thought that the ironic brilliance of aesthetic realism fosters a paucity of human commitment, if it is felt that Hemingway sold the Romantic self short, if irony itself is viewed as the emblem of a Bohemian intransigence which the writer can no longer afford—whether he feels that there is no viable Bohemian community or he feels that identification with our most characteristic suffering is the way of transcending it—it is a tribute to him that a number of our recent novelists, Norman Mailer and Saul Bellow for example, still think of him as an angel to wrestle with, a father to kill. Considering the narrowness, even the exclusiveness, of his vision, it has had considerable endurance, attributable in good measure to the fact that he made his encounter with literature an inextricable part of it.

Robert Evans

Hemingway and the Pale Cast of Thought

The charge that Hemingway is an "anti-intellectual" writer has, in one formulation or another, echoed through some decades of criticism and, by dint of much repetition, has emerged as a critical commonplace. It is a characteristic often observed of commonplaces that they are much asserted and little examined. By a tacit gentlemen's agreement they are granted a sort of diplomatic immunity to search and scrutiny, and not the least consequence of this is that they may smuggle into critical discussions meanings which their users neither recognize nor intend. Further, their use often conveys to the unwary a greater sense of unanimity and certainty than may in truth exist. Thus, those who glory in Hemingway's "anti-intellectualism" and those who deplore it seem equally to affirm it, to endow it with all the solidity of fact. There is, I believe, one very important sense in which Hemingway's work is clearly anti-intellectual, and I wish to consider this in some detail. There are a number of other senses in which this charge is either false or else trivial and irrelevant. I shall dismiss these latter briefly, but with the cautionary note that, for all their flimsiness, they have been the central props in many a discussion of Hemingway's work, and their influence remains out of all proportion to their validity.

For those critics who cannot resist the seductions of the biographical approach, Hemingway's private life affords many examples of anti-intellectual behavior. His celebrated quarrel with Max Eastman, his declared contempt for Proust and Mann, the color and violence of his recreations—each has added its brush stroke to the portrait of the artist as anti-intellectual, and the hirsute barrel-chest, the grizzled pre-beatnik beard, the scars of old wounds have likewise been pressed into the service of the legend.

The superficiality of this "evidence" and its irrelevance to any reasoned judgment of Hemingway's work are so apparent that all who run may read, and I do not propose to belabor a dead horse. Attempts are still made to saddle the old jade and flog it into the arena of criticism, but the beast's ribs all show, and in such blatant displays as these mere recognition suffices for refutation. More persuasive, and hence more frequently encountered, are those arguments in which the facts of Hemingway's private life are discreetly manipulated to give coloring and tonality to a discussion purporting to be of the works themselves, usually with copious parallels drawn, or hinted, between the works and the biographical data. Not infrequently the question of "primitivism" is adroitly raised, and we are reminded that Hemingway has portrayed, as Edgar Johnson puts it, "simple and ignorant people: prize fighters, matadors, boys, jockeys, whores, bartenders, waiters." But the devoted craftsman whose work was blue-penciled by Pound and Stein was not aesthetically a primitive at all,[1] and his characters, often simple, ignorant, and socially marginal types to be sure, can easily be matched in these respects by many of those of Dostoevsky, Dickens and Zola.

Basically correct, the charge that Hemingway is an anti-intellectual (in a sense to be defined shortly) rests not upon his personal life and character, nor upon the characters in his books, but upon a total attitude which shapes and controls those characters, limits their experience and their responses to it, and emerges finally as a more or less consciously held position in which mind and imagination are deprecated and the qualities of animal courage and endurance ("holding tight") are extolled.

In this, Hemingway by no means stands outside the historical currents of his time. Except for the quite recent prominence of the "Ox-bridge" analytical school, the philosophies of this century, especially as they have filtered into popular thought and literature, have stressed qualities other than those congenial to a rational humanism. Cases in point are Bergsonian intuitionism, which deprecates mind as an unfortunate limiting agent; pragmatism, which has its locus in action and the results of action; the once popular crude Watsonian behaviorism and its more refined replacement, positivism; phenomenology, with its abdication of all interpretation and evaluation; and existentialism, with its concern for certain emotional states. In Hemingway's writing we can

---

[1] There is a sense, anthropological rather than aesthetic, in which the term is applicable and which has some bearing on our subsequent discussion of emotion and action in Hemingway's work. See Malcolm Cowley's introduction to the Viking Portable *Hemingway* (New York, 1944), pp. xviii–xxiii.

identify the fragments of now one, now another of these systems of thought. Witness the existential despair of "A Clean, Well-Lighted Place," or the extreme, and extremely naïve, ethical pragmatism of such an assertion as, "I know only that what is moral is what you feel good after and what is immoral is what you feel bad after."[2] Even the celebrated Hemingway style, with its austere refusal to comment and its scrupulous fidelity to objective detail, is—to a certain degree—the literary equivalent of behaviorism and phenomenology.

I

These, though little more than straws in the wind, nevertheless suggest a writer who finds congenial subject matter in intense emotional states, who approaches ethics by the rather meandering and uncertain path of the feelings, and who, using language to fix and define an objective reality, does so not because that reality is to be matter for subsequent intellectual investigation, but because, thus fixed and defined, it will generate an aesthetically valued emotion, for what Hemingway "was working very hard to try to get," he tells us, was "the sequence of motion and fact which made the emotion" that he wanted to communicate through his stories.[3]

Now concern for emotion is by no means suspect in itself, nor is it necessarily incompatible with a highly intellectual temper, but in Hemingway's work, emotion plays a role scarcely paralleled in the works of any other contemporary writer. In most fiction, a character's actions either emerge directly from his emotions, which they unambiguously express, or, more interestingly, action is emotion whose expression is modified by external pressures or by the character's recognition of values and goals that must take precedence over his emotions. Oversimplified as this statement is, it will yet serve to make clear the radical contrast between the traditional relationship of action and emotion and that prevailing in Hemingway's fiction, for with Hemingway there is a profound discontinuity between emotion and action. Action is not the outward thrust of emotion which, however much modified, gives the stamp of integrity to the character's expression of himself in his world. The crucial and distinctive action in Hemingway's fiction is directed inward; it is repressive, not expressive, and it functions primarily as a means for containing and making bearable emotion of a peculiarly destructive sort. To accomplish this, the action

[2] Ernest Hemingway, *Death in the Afternoon* (New York, 1932), p. 4.
[3] *Ibid.,* p. 2.

need not be violent and painful, though often it is. An enormous concentration on the trivial and routine—going fishing, having a drink—will do just as well. What matters is the total absorptive power of the action, its capacity for temporarily annihilating or insulating the attention. This accounts for the remarkably disturbing stillness of the surface of those stories in which "nothing seems to happen." It is the stillness of a powerful spring drawn to the breaking point, so that release or the slightest additional tension must equally result in violence; and the reader, sensing this perilous equilibrium in which all the resources of the protagonist are stretched to their limits, knows that disaster can be staved off for only so long, and that already time has nearly run out.

The relation of all this to our view of Hemingway as an anti-intellectual writer is not far to seek. The normal triad of thought, emotion, and action is reduced in Hemingway's work by the deliberate excision of the most typically human and civilized member of the three, and in the fictional world that results, the characters continually require the opiate of action to dull their awareness of emotions that fester inward—emotions, we should perhaps add, which only thought might lance and drain. It becomes possible now to identify quite precisely the most striking and characteristic feature of Hemingway's anti-intellectualism. It is not at all the blunt man-of-action's cheerful contempt for the subtle, tentative indirections of the man of thought; much less is it a joyous Lawrencian affirmation of the dark powers of blood and sex as against the dry light of the mind. It is instead an act of calculated retrenchment, involving a deliberate refusal to admit the free play of the higher intellectual faculties—reason, speculative thought, and imaginative vision—as legitimate guides for conduct and as potential means for clarifying, ordering, and enriching human experience.[4]

II

This was not a position that Hemingway arrived at gradually, as some writers, by stages, work their way to some final affirmation or despair. His anti-intellectualism was brought *to* his writing,

[4] Philip Young, in his short but penetrating study, *Ernest Hemingway* (New York, 1952), suggests a reason for this attitude, and to Young's book I have a large general indebtedness. In this article, however, I am interested not in pursuing the personal psychology of Hemingway, which Young has already treated so perceptively, but in addressing myself to the work itself, in isolating there those *loci critici* which will help to define the distinctive features of Hemingway's anti-intellectualism, and in assessing the work in terms of the philosophy it espouses.

not discovered through it, and far from abandoning or moderating this attitude as the years passed, he became both more explicit and more insistent in proclaiming it.

As early as 1925, with *In Our Time,* Hemingway had discovered how important it is not to think. The story "Big Two-Hearted River," included in this volume, has long been recognized as quintessential Hemingway, and like much of his best work it communicates largely through implication. Considerable latitude therefore exists for difference of opinions as to precisely what it is the story implies. The reader cannot, however, be deaf to the sinister resonance of the references to the swamp and the "tragic fishing" that awaits Nick Adams there, nor can he ignore the closing statement that "there were plenty of days coming when [Nick] could fish the swamp." The shadows that lie just beyond the close of the story are not the only ones that by their (implied) presence set in sharp relief the ordered detail of the story and put the finest possible edge on the contours of event and thing. There is an antecedent area of shadow as well, out of which the hero moves into the bright midsummer focus of this story. It may be no more than a cloud, "no bigger than a man's hand," perhaps, but it is there, and it is a relief to escape it. "Nick was happy," we are told at the beginning of the story, and the very next sentence tells us why. "He felt he had left everything behind, the need for thinking, the need to write, other needs. It was all back of him." But of course it will not remain back of him. The end of the story leaves no doubt on that score, and furthermore "it," the dark cluster or clot of needs, foremost of which is the need for thinking, threatens at one point to intrude and cast its shadow upon Nick's moral holiday.

The context of this intrusion is important. It comes at the end of the first day, before the fishing begins and before the wilderness has had time fully to isolate Nick from all the things he wanted to leave behind. Nick has pitched camp and had supper, and now he is making coffee, the last thing he will do before turning in for the night. Making coffee calls up memories of someone named Hopkins, and for two full paragraphs a writer justly noted for economy and highly selective detail allows his protagonist to reminisce about his relationship with Hopkins. The relationship had been close: "He had once argued about everything with Hopkins," and it had apparently been affectionate as well, for—deliberately and even sentimentally—Nick makes the coffee just as Hopkins always did: "He would not let it steep in the pot at all. Not the first cup. It should be straight Hopkins all the way. Hop deserved that." But Hopkins struck it rich and went away, though promising to come back: "They were all going fishing again next summer. . . . He would get a yacht and they would all cruise along the north shore of Lake Superior." But for whatever reasons, never known, the promise was not kept, and "they never saw Hopkins again." By this point in the reminiscing, the coffee was ready:

> Nick drank the coffee, the coffee according to Hopkins. The coffee was bitter. Nick laughed. It made a good ending to the story. His mind was starting to work. He knew he could choke it because he was tired enough.[5]

It is quite clear that the statement that Nick's mind was starting to work is by no means irrelevant at this point, nor does it cut violently across the line of the story. Indeed, it *is* the line of the story, and it flows by both an intellectual and an emotional logic directly out of the events that precede it. Neither Cowley nor Young seems to have noticed this. The former speaks rather vaguely of Nick's trying to escape from "nightmares or . . . realities that have become a nightmare,"[6] and the latter observes that Nick is "desperately protecting his mind against whatever it is that he is escaping."[7] But there is no need to say "whatever it is," for the text makes it plain enough that Nick is trying to suppress certain fully dramatized bitter memories that end in bitter laughter. And the bitter cup, the gospel according to Hopkins, is nothing less than the age-old draught of loss, betrayal, and a broken promise. It is the remembrance of these things that stirs heavily within him, like a powerful motor beginning to turn over. These are the wounds that ache as the night closes in, and Nick has come young to his share of them.[8]

Two further points should be made about this specific passage. One concerns the relationship established there between

[5] Cowley, p. 476.

[6] *Ibid.,* p. x.

[7] Young, p. 17.

[8] We might add that, in common with all of Hemingway's wounded heroes, Nick maintains an essentially subjective relationship to his "wound"; that is, he is passive, *pathētos:* he suffers his wound, but he never attempts to prove it, to objectify it, to come to terms with it intellectually. The wound is sealed away in some dimension of mental space which is never willingly entered, but for that very reason it gains an irresistible power to enter—indeed, invade—the hero's consciousness, as fresh and painful as ever. If Hemingway's works fall short of tragedy—and I think that more of them do than is generally supposed—the reason is to be sought precisely here: in the hero's persistent refusal to explore that one area of his being where he might encounter himself in his most secret and terrifying terms. There is an ultimate failure in confrontation; a failure, ironically enough, of nerve; and even death is seized, not as a final illumination, but as the last possible means of self-evasion and escape.

thought and action; the other concerns the nature of thought itself, and the limitations Hemingway places upon it both here and in the rest of his fiction. To take these points in order: Nick's mind starts working, but he knows he can choke it *because he is tired.* Even at the beginning of his career, in his first major book, Hemingway opposes the thrust of thought with the counter-thrust of action: carrying a heavy pack for miles uphill on a hot day, pitching camp, stowing your gear away—sheer, draining physical activity—this is the great thought-preventive, the central weapon in the unremitting warfare against the mind. Other weapons soon came to hand and were as quickly seized—drinking, the violent distractions of sex, war, hunting—but these are really no more than variations on the primary theme of action, which remained unchanged, and which was present from the first.

It remains only to note that the mental activity which is stifled in this episode is not that of reason and speculative thought. What Nick Adams is struggling against pre-eminently is *recollection,* the recall of past and hence unalterable experience with its charge of unalterable pain. The words "thought" and "thinking" do not occur here, but if I may anticipate my evidence, the activity Nick tries to choke is precisely what Hemingway elsewhere labels "thinking." "To think," in Hemingway's lexicon, has two primary meanings. One is to remember; the other to worry. Whenever we find one of his characters struggling not to think, the text can invariably be glossed with one or the other of these meanings. If this is correct, and I believe that subsequent examples will confirm it, then we could ask for no more damning evidence of the anti-intellectual bias that characterizes Hemingway's fiction. In effect, Hemingway wipes out the distinction between thought and emotion and makes of thought only a subspecies of unpleasant emotion, for both worry and that sort of memory which the Hemingway hero tries to repress are characterized by ineffectual preoccupation with circumstances which cannot be altered and by an accompanying inner distress and pain. Small wonder that the protagonist flees from such "thought" to the bright fields of danger, where he can at least encounter the immediacies of sensation and deed! But nowhere in Hemingway's work does there glimmer even the faintest suggestion that one's life can be ordered by thought, or that it is at all desirable to attempt such an ordering. No generous or comprehensive notion of the place of thought in human affairs emerges from his work. Thought is always the wound, never the physician. Practical thought, the choice and supervision of shrewdly calculated trains of action that lead to a concrete goal, is abundantly present in Hemingway's fiction. What is lacking is any parallel in the realm of speculative thought. Significantly and characteristically, the Hemingway hero lacks the intellectual resources to achieve a distance from his suffering, to contemplate it, and to learn from it something fundamental about himself. He is thus condemned always to relive his experience, without ever mastering either it or its lessons.

For Whom the Bell Tolls, involving war, love, Spain, and death—all things close to Hemingway's rogue-male heart—marks in various ways a terminus in its author's career. With the completion of this novel, his significant contribution to American fiction was behind him. His most memorable characters had been created, his typical themes had been discovered and explored, and his style, lean and a bit staccato in the beginning, had, without losing its old virtues, achieved a broader range of effects. There remained ahead of him only the overvalued and too heavily symbolic tale *The Old Man and the Sea,* the justly condemned *Across the River and into the Trees,* and the living out of a life that had already become legend.

This watershed novel, then, provides an ideal test case for establishing the persistence and centrality in Hemingway's work of an anti-intellectual bias. The support it gives to this charge is almost overwhelming in its abundance and in its forthrightness of statement. As early as the eighth page of the novel Hemingway begins to hammer at the dangers of thought. Golz, the general who sends Robert Jordan on his mission, says to Jordan: "I never think at all. Why should I? I am *Général Sovietique.* I never think. Do not try to trap me into thinking." But it is not only Soviet generals who regard thinking as a trap to be avoided. During the conversation, Jordan finds himself thinking about the attack which will come, but abruptly he shifts:

> He would not think about that. That was not his business. That was Golz's business. He had only one thing to do and that was what he should think about and he must think it out clearly and take everything as it came along, and not worry. To worry was as bad as to be afraid. It simply made things more difficult.[9]

This passage is important for two reasons. First, it points up the previously mentioned distinction which Hemingway draws between speculative and practical thought, presented here in the contrast between "thinking about" something and "thinking [something] out." The preposition and the adverb illuminate almost miraculously the attitudes held toward the two modes of thinking,

[9] *For Whom the Bell Tolls* (New York, 1940), pp. 8–9.

the one tied to its object, bumbling uselessly round and about without ever getting free of it, the other flashing arrow-like straight from the thought to its goal, out! Out of the maze! Practical thought, the application of mind to the solution of specific problems, is clearly legitimate. What is objected to—and this will later become even more obvious—is speculative thought, the giving over of the mind to the comtemplation of those endless chains of reaction and consequence, both material and moral, which attend upon all human actions. Secondly, the passage is important because it subtly links thought to worry. Just as Jordan shouldn't think about these things, so too he shouldn't worry about them. This semi-equation of speculative thought and worry appears throughout the novel, and the cumulative effect is to degrade a serious and uniquely human attribute to the level of mere fretting, to the incessant pawing of a wild animal at the door of its cage.

Only a few pages later, Jordan is again cautioning himself against thinking:

> He'd certainly been solemn and gloomy with Golz. The job had overwhelmed him a little. . . . Golz was gay and he had wanted him to be gay too before he left, but he hadn't been.
>
> All the best ones, when you thought it over, were gay. . . . There were not many of them left though. No, there were not many of the gay ones left. There were very damned few of them left. And if you keep on thinking like that, my boy, you won't be left either. Turn off the thinking now, old timer, old comrade. You're a bridge-blower now. Not a thinker.[10]

Here the absence of thought is marked by a certain enviable gaiety of spirit in Golz, whereas Jordan, who is thinking too much, is gloomy. But not only is one happier if one doesn't think; one is also safer: "If you keep on thinking like that, my boy, you won't be left either." Thought is thus portrayed as inimical to action, or at least to the successful completion of an action.

Other characters besides Golz and Jordan illustrate the dangers of thought and its tendency to spoil action. Kashkin, the dynamiter, is an almost classic example of the man made sick by thinking too precisely on the event. He could not help thinking (= worrying) about all the possibilities of failure, the chances of being captured and tortured. Eventually (one is tempted to say, consequently), there is a failure, and to escape what he had thought so much about, he persuades Jordan to kill him. (Kashkin has "a prejudice against killing himself.") It is obviously very bad form, and moreover, his attitude, communicated to the guerrillas,

[10] *Ibid.,* p. 17.

definitely subverts the value of what he did manage to accomplish. In one laconic phrase, Jordan at once sums up and passes judgment on Kashkin's compulsion to think: "it spoiled his work."[11]

If Kashkin illustrates the danger of thought in the sense of "worry," Pilar, in the following quotation, illustrates the pain attendant upon thought in its other sense, "memory." She has been telling Jordan of the mass murder of the Fascists in her town, and when the last atrocity has been narrated, she says: "Then I went back inside the room and I sat there and I did not wish to think for that was the worst day of my life. . . ."[12]

It is more than a little like Nick Adams in "The Killers," when he comes face to face with the knowledge that Ole is going to be murdered: "I can't stand to think about him waiting in the room and knowing he's going to get it. It's too damned awful." And George gives the solution which (in 1927) is already standard Hemingway, and will remain so: "Well . . . you better not think about it."

One or two more passages should suffice to illustrate the extent to which an unconcealed antagonism to thought permeates *For Whom the Bell Tolls*. Jordan, after he has found Maria, broods over the little time they have left together:

> In sickness and in health. Till death do us part. In two nights. . . . Much more than likely and now lay off that sort of thinking. You can stop that now. That's not good for you. Do nothing that is not good for you.[13]

Once again thought is rendered suspect; it is "not good for you." Do not do what is not good for you. Therefore, do not think. "My mind is in suspension until we win the war," Jordan says, and again we encounter the familiar notion of a specific physical action to be performed and the clear-cut implication that thought would interfere with the successful completion of this action.

It might be objected that, after all, Jordan *is* engaged in a war, in which swift and unhampered action is crucial. What is more understandable, then, that he should forego the luxuries of speculation and keep himself, "for the duration," as free from the grit of thought as the well-oiled mechanism of a rifle? It is a familiar argument, and a shameless one. It is, in its most clear-cut form, the position of the anti-intellectual, who pays lip service to thought as long as there is no occasion for action, or when the issues in-

[11] *Ibid.,* p. 171.
[12] *Ibid.,* p. 129.
[13] *Ibid.,* p. 168.

volved do not touch him deeply, but who is ready to cast it away on the instant, like a dry shuck, the moment a really "important" matter arises. Distrustful of thought, impatient of its austere commitment to scrutiny, to the painstaking weighing not only of means but of ends, such a person clamors incessantly for action, as though in it, and it alone, salvation lay. War may indeed call ordinary values into question, but it does not leave them so. By inverting our everyday awareness and thrusting death vividly into the foreground, it places in the sharpest possible relief all values, true and false, and thus heightens our perception of those things that are truly good and of lasting worth. For some men, and Hemingway is of their number, thought comes out a poor second, and in its stead the virtues of animal courage and endurance are set up. It is not to these virtues that we should object, but to their exclusiveness, to the insistence that thought is pernicious, and to the implication that the world is so truly narrowed that these are the only values possible for an honest man to hold.

At one point, late in the novel, Jordan's thoughts turn to his father, who had committed suicide because, Jordan says, he was a coward and could not endure the torture of a nagging wife. Then:

> You better not think at all, he told himself. Soon you will be with Maria and you won't have to think. That's the best way now that everything is worked out. When you have been concentrating so hard on something you can't stop and your brain gets to racing like a flywheel with the weight gone. You better just not think.[14]

It is the final position, to which Hemingway has tended all along in his writing, the absolute and unqualified rejection of thought: "You better not think at all. . . . You better just not think." Further, the occasion for this passage—the hero's refusal (or inability) to consider rationally certain painful areas of his experience—suggests the fundamental objection to thought in Hemingway's work: thinking forces us to come to grips, in what may prove a death struggle, with a world too vicious and brutal for us to endure. That way madness lies. Do not think; and though things won't go away (we've tried that before), still they can't get through to hurt us.

III

This is perhaps sufficient to demonstrate the extent to which a vigorous and clearly stated antagonism to thought pervades *For*

[14] *Ibid.,* p. 340.

Whom the Bell Tolls, the work which, as we have already observed, brings to a close the first and by far the most significant period in Hemingway's career. I wish now to consider briefly how certain other elements in his work relate to this fundamental attitude, and then to criticize the attitude itself and the Hemingway world which it so imperiously governs.

What have long been recognized as standard fixtures in the Hemingway world—the sex, drinking, hunting, bullfighting, and other acts of violence—are all essentially therapeutic: they are thought-preventives; and thoughts, for Hemingway, are not "the immortal progenie of glorie excellent" but things that come in the night when you can't sleep, "when your brain gets to racing like a flywheel with the weight gone." They are giants that hurt and cripple, and the best thing to do is not to think but to take a shot of giant-killer. These acts of violence, as often as not directed inward upon the self rather than outward upon others, are thus not extrinic and isolable elements. They are intimately related to that fear and distrust of thought which is at the core of Hemingway's anti-intellectualism. Further, this anti-intellectualism itself is not to be explained as the shameless display of a hairy chest and gorilla-mentality, but rather as the self-imposed discipline of one living in a community of violence and pain, one to whom thought plus imagination equals fear. It is an attempt to come to terms with reality, to render at least some meaningful activity possible; and, applied as widely as it is in Hemingway's novels and stories, this discipline becomes, in effect, a philosophy.

The reader of fiction, unless he asks no more than diversion, must sooner or later disengage himself from the work to which he had provisionally surrendered his own perception of art and life and, having effected this separation, must judge where before he felt. The judgment of Hemingway's fiction has been beset with more than ordinary difficulties, but this test does not exempt us from the obligation to judge. I do not pretend that it is all to do. A large body of first-rate Hemingway criticism already exists, a number of more or less definitive insights have been arrived at, and I doubt strongly whether any posthumously appearing work of Hemingway's will *significantly* alter our present understanding and evaluation of his work. Evaluation of the literary artifact may proceed under either or both of two modes: aesthetic, or moral and intellectual, to the extent that these latter may profitably be separated from the former. This article is frankly concerned with the moral and intellectual, and in particular it has been concerned with what I have called anti-intellectualism in Hemingway's fiction. This term is not as precise as I should like, yet it will do as a convenient rubric under which to subsume the gross and persistent reduction of thought to worry or painful memory, the reiterated charge that thought hinders rather than abets action (which is consistently accorded pride of place), and the whole complex of varied distrusts and antagonisms manifested toward thought in all of Hemingway's major works.

Though most of these elements have been noted before, it has usually been in passing, and they have never been fully explored or articulated; nor has there been any forthright judgment of Hemingway's work based on the anti-intellectualism per se displayed there. The emphasis has invariably been either on the role of action in his work or on the painful experiences and emotions that are presumed to justify the relentless denial of thought. It is this too one-sided emphasis that I wish to redress here, and I shall begin by asserting flatly how remarkably boring and narrow much of the Hemingway world is. There are vast reaches of moral, intellectual, aesthetic, and even social experience that are forever beyond anyone penned hopelessly in these novels by the author's private geography of despair. The felt need for a tight control has restricted disastrously the area over which that control must be exercised, and though the Hemingway hero may move with a firm and directed footstep, it is across a bleak and impoverished landscape that he makes his way.

The canvas seems deceptively wide—the Caribbean, Paris, Spain, Africa—and yet there is a remarkable sameness to these landscapes, because they are inhabited and animated by people who suffer from the same problems—boredom, futility, obsession with some never fully explored or explained inner despair—and when they react to these problems, they react in a pathetically same way and try to find solutions in acts of violence, in sex, in alcohol. It is a repetitive world and, finally, a drearily predictable one, whose ultimate wisdom attains to no more than "Hold tight; and above all, don't think."

A brief comparison with Faulkner is suggestive. In Hemingway's stories or novels, taken individually, the social world (to the extent we are made aware of society at all) is usually homogeneous. The major characters either belong to the same station, or, if not, the difference between them is effectively abrogated by some extraordinary situation such as a war, or else the usual and manifest social pressures simply fail to enter the story in any meaningful way. Faulkner's world is frankly hierarchical. His society has structure, points of definition, lines of demarcation, but the structure is not frozen, and the action in his novels often arises out of the characters' attempts to achieve a new social definition (the

Snopes Clan) or to preserve intact manners and attitudes no longer adequate to the changing times (Col. Sartoris, Gail Hightower, Miss Emily). A compelling sense of history operates in all of Faulkner's major works, giving density and resonance to the actions narrated. Time, as the tragic dimension through which men are obliged to move, is fully accepted, and that acceptance lends a sober dignity to his work. With Hemingway, no sense of history is evident even in those novels where it would be most expected: *A Farewell to Arms* and *For Whom the Bell Tolls.* His characters almost invariably live and act in the specious present. They are drifters, physically and spiritually, and for drifters the time is always now. The past is rejected, because in it lurk things too ugly or painful to contemplate, and the future involves precisely that exercise of speculative thought which Hemingway's work so consistently denies.

Even the style of the two men helps to illuminate this basic difference in attitude. Faulkner's rhetoric, for all its verbal *panache,* contrasted with the tight, pulled-down sentences of Hemingway, suggests that he is not afraid of letting go, and that, moreover, certain things exist—values, traditions, ideals—that are worth pulling out all the stops for. Hemingway is suspicious of rhetoric (not wholly without reason, we must admit); abstract words such as "glory, honor, courage" no longer seem to have meaning, he tells us in a celebrated passage. He prefers to know the names of places and what the weather was like. But perhaps these words, and others like them, have lost their meanings in the very act of the novelist's definition of his world, in his ruthless stripping of things to the here and now. A world devoid of a sense of history and time, of past actions and future consequences, of speculative thought and imaginative vision, is not a human world at all. It is an animal world, a world of weathers and immediate sensations. It is not surprising, then, in such a world, that language and the values funded in language become suspect and embarrassing.

The other signal defect of this anti-intellectualism is, as might be expected, its emotional immaturity. The giants that stalk Hemingway's world are experiences never measured and subdued by thought, never ordered within a framework of existence more comprehensive than that of a rather sensitive adolescent. The path to wisdom, Katherine Anne Porter reminds us, is downward, and the steep descent is haunted by specters we would rather not face, but must. But Hemingway's heroes refuse to grapple openly with these specters of cruelty, intolerance, pain, betrayal, vileness —all the unsounded nightside of our mysterious and imperfect nature. To borrow a figure of Melville's, they cannot or dare not strike through the pasteboard masks to the reality and the terror behind. Theirs is the fugitive and cloistered virtue that does not seek its adversary but slinks out of the race, leaving the trial and victory to another.

This may seem a strange, even an impertinent criticism of an author whose works are so full of pain and violence, and full, too, of men who with a courageous endurance perform some dangerous action which circumstance has made imperative. But these heroes are in fact moral cripples who have retrenched to the limit and are fighting, on their own ground and their own terms, evils which—however bad they may seem—are less terrible than those from which they flee. Thus, their action is not the triumphant banishing of specters; it is only a substitute for nightmare. We must pity such men, but we need not take them as models for emulation; and before we accept the Hemingway world and ethic, and praise them as "manly" or "realistic," we should be quite sure that we are willing to accept courage that will not face the real enemy and action which does not solve the real problem as being just as good as the real thing. For all its blood and thunder, Hemingway's world is not quite man-sized.

Philip Young

The World and an American Myth

> *An obsession with evil, early sorrow and death appears astonishingly native to the American muse. "Whatever the American men of genius are," an English critic observed, "they are not young gods making a young world."—Matthew Josephson*

Every true novelist has a "world" of some kind, an imaginary vision of some sphere or scene of life and action which his individual experience has caused him to see, and which he re-creates in fiction. This is his equivalent for what, if he wrote philosophy, would be a system of ideas. He sees a kind of life going against some background, and he tries to make it coherent and dramatic. He induces us to see it all through his eyes, and after we have done this we ask ourselves questions about the breadth of his vision and the depth of his perspective. We ask if this is a "real" world, one we can recognize and accept as true.

The pattern of Hemingway's coherence is plain and for the most part dramatic. His vision and its texture make up his world. This world is the world of Missouri transformed first into the world of northern Michigan. Indians replace Negroes as primitives who exist outside the bounds of middle-class ways, where life is in the raw, and feuds and jackknife Caesareans are possible. It is a place overlaid with a distorting respectability that forces an escape, which is an escape to pain. And then this place is itself transformed to a European battleground, where violence is organized on a grand scale into the formalized brutality of war.

Hemingway's world is ultimately a world at war—war either in the literal sense of armed and calculated conflict, or figuratively as marked everywhere with violence, potential or present, and a general hostility. In his view of it the hillside is pocked with shell

holes, the branch of the tree is shattered, the highway is clogged
with soldiers, trucks, refugees and carts, and the daughter of the
innkeeper has been raped.

The people of this world operate under such conditions—
desperation, apprehension, emergency, stiff-lipped fear and
pleasure seized in haste— as are imposed by war. Their ordeals are
by fire; manhood is attained under it, and womanhood is tested
by its courageous acceptance. The old are scarred and have the
wisdom of their wounds; the young are off somewhere learning,
awaiting their turn. The brave are the fair. In the background are
the walking wounded, the special figures of those who have survived their ordeals and come to some adjustment—the matadors
and gamblers and fighters and deep-sea fishermen. Behind them
are those who did not survive and readjust—the physical, intellectual and moral cripples, the stretcher cases; the bereaved, the
doped and the queer. Emerging from them are the hero: a soldier,
struck down but returned to duty, gear packed, ready to move.
And the heroine: the girl the soldier can meet, love and part from
forever in a space of days spent in some foreign city. They leave
no children behind them. They leave nothing behind them but
empty bottles and the signature in the register; when they are gone
they exist only in the short memories of the tipped—the desk
clerk, the waiter and the elevator boy. They are going to lose and
they know it, but they can delay what is inevitable with the special
knowledge that hazard teaches and by a decent respect for
mystery. A shadow envelops them, which is the shadow of death,
the essential preoccupation of those who live close to the front.

Restricted grimly by the urgencies of war, their morality is
harshly pragmatic: what's moral is what you feel good after. Related to this is their code, which summarizes the virtues of the
soldier. It is tested by conduct in the face of death; it is the ethic
of wartime. And it operates, in a way, off-duty, for when the soldier
is not at war he is in escape of it—on leave or, at the very least,
in the reserve. And escaping this world is but to imitate it: one
kills, instead of other soldiers, ducks, marlin, kudu, lions, bulls and
horses. This escape functions to keep alive the conditions escaped,
until the real things come back. In despite of alcohol the muscles
stay hard, the reflexes quick and the eye clear against the day
when once more it is not in fun, and the target shoots back. The
activities of escape go according to the rules of sport, which
make up the code of the armistice, the temporary, peacetime
modification of the rules of war.

As the exigencies of warfare obliterate the niceties of moral
considerations, so a state of war limits the soldier pretty much to

those pleasures which the senses communicate. Peril heightens his awareness of his senses, and privation enhances their gratification. The pleasures of taste and touch predominate, and the hero is like all soldiers in that women, food and drink supply all that he values beyond the code.

Hemingway's world is one in which things do not grow and bear fruit, but explode, break, decompose, or are eaten away. It is saved from total misery by visions of endurance, by what happiness the body can give when it does not hurt, by interludes of love which cannot outlast the furlough and by a pleasure in the landscapes of countries and cafés one can visit. A man has dignity only as he can walk with a courage that has no purpose beyond itself among the fellow wounded, with an ear alert for the sound of the shell that really has his number on it. It is a barren world of fragments which lies before us like a land of bad dreams, where a few pathetic idylls and partial triumphs relieve the diet of nightmare. It has neither light nor love that lasts nor certitude nor peace nor much help for pain. It is swept with the actualities of struggle and flight, and up ahead in the darkness the armies are engaged.

Of course it is easy to protest this world. It is a world seen through a crack in a wall by a man who is pinned down by gunfire, who can move outside to look around only on penalty of the death he seeks but also seeks to stay. Missing from it is a very large part of what our own eyes have also seen. There is a farmhouse down the road. The farmer was born there and has lived there all his life. His daughter, who was never raped, has married, had children and moved to town. Most of these people will never see a kudu or a bullfight, and war for them is a thing to be wholly avoided or, failing that, forgot with the discharge papers. Hemingway's world is a narrow one, which is real to us in a limited and partial way only, for he has left out of it a great deal of what many people would quite simply call "life." And his view of his world is not much less restricted. Nowhere in this writer can you find the mature, brooding intelligence, the sense of the past, the grown-up relationships of adult people, and many of the other things we normally ask of a first-rate novelist. Only battles, or their preludes or aftermaths, and Hemingway hypnotized by the one note he sounds. Only a tiny cast of characters, who change their names, but never represent more than a tiny minority of the people we have known. This vision is eccentric and verges on psychosis. It is violence-obsessed. The gaze is a glassy-eyed stare at what is or soon will be a corpse. It insists that we honor a stubborn and nearly hysterical preoccupation with the profound significance of violence in our time.

We do not do badly to protest Hemingway's world. It is not
the one we wish to live in, and we usually believe that indeed we
do not live in it. It is not a world, ultimately, in which some of us
are even very interested. But if we should look back over our time,
what facts could we choose to stack against the facts of violence,
evil and death? We remember countless "minor" wars, and two
major slaughters, and prepare for a third holocaust beyond which
we cannot see anything or at all. We count casualties by the millions and run out of fingers, appropriate billions and can see no
end to it. We may argue the utter inadequacy of the world Hemingway refracted and re-created. It is a hell of a world, and we should
protest it. But on the other hand we should be hard pressed to
prove that it is not the one we inhabit.

It is still too early to know which of all the worlds our writers
offer will be the ones we shall turn out to have lived in. It all
depends on what happens, and you never know at the time. But it
is not too early to make predictions on the basis of the evidence
that is already available, and there is enough of that to back Hemingway's world as strongly as the world constructed by any other
twentieth-century American. It is a gloomy guess, but what we
call a "good" one, that while other writers were watching the side
acts, Hemingway's eyes were from the start riveted on the main
show. "Peace in our time" was an obscure and ironic prophecy.
But it was stated at the very beginning and stuck to, and it was a
brilliant prophecy, as our bad luck would have it.

Our bad luck is not necessarily a writer's, who has an iron in
the fire that we do not, a future that passes over his death as if it
did not matter. Among other people, this kind of future belongs to
writers who have written prose which will still be "valid in a year or
in ten years or, with luck and if you stated it purely enough,
always." It is hard to think that some things could be stated more
purely than Hemingway stated them; there are passages in him
which, given his purposes and preconceptions, cannot be im-
proved. It is harder to know about "luck," or even what it means.
Still, there are ways in which Hemingway may be said to have often
had it. He frequently showed a kind of sixth sense for relevance,
for seizing on the exact mood of the moment and expressing it.
But more striking is the stroke of his wounding, which fixed his
attention permanently on his subject. The series of accidents
which began up in Michigan and was climaxed at Fossalta restricted Hemingway to a world that a rational choice might never have
hit on.

It was not long ago that we thought other worlds than Hemingway's were the true ones. These worlds were, speaking loosely,

"social" or "psychological." They were built of Main Streets and "the American scene" for a while, and then of cities and factory towns and their workers. Or they were built on insights provided by a new psychology, and investigated the complexities of human personality. As far as both groups were concerned, war was an utter tragedy, yes, but it was a thing we knew better than to get involved in any more. Once a hatred for it had been firmly expressed, it became really a kind of bore, and to write about it was juvenile or cheap. War was a kind of odd irrelevance to the serious concerns of the age.

But we have lived to see all this look silly when set for significance beside the breakdown of peace in our century. It is quite possible that Hemingway, with all his obvious limitations, has been saying the truest things of our age truly, and these are materials for the building of permanent reputations. The early up-in-Michigan stories bespoke a vision of the public future that was chillingly accurate. It would be simple timidity not to predict that the private visions of "Kilimanjaro" and *The Old Man* were just as clear.

Prose fiction has characters, a style, a setting and a story to tell. Hemingway's characters we have met. His style and its origins and effects we have had a look at. We have abstracted and judged his world, and retold his story. There is nothing superficial about his vision, however narrow it may be. But when the adventures of his hero are placed as they ought to be beside those of Huck Finn, they may be made to say something profound. When a story is told in such a way as Twain told his, and it sticks and we return to it to find it always fresh and moving, we may be pretty sure that something is being said that we have an interest in hearing. When the story is told again, in a way befitting its own time, and literate Americans follow it and are moved again, we can be positive that it has more than a passing significance for us. The story of Huck and the Hemingway hero says some very basic things about what it is like to live in America.

First of all we can see that the ordeals of Mark Twain and Ernest Hemingway and their protagonists are excellent examples for the anonymous Englishman who wished to point out that our men of genius have assuredly not been young gods making a young world. And yet this is the reverse of what we often assume. We have a long tradition that prepares that assumption, and *Huckleberry Finn* has often been thought a part of it. Vachel Lindsay once wrote that Huck is the "American race," and that race the "new childhood of the world." We frequently think of this country as being still in the spring of life.

In a way it is true. Some years ago, during an investigation of Communist activity in Hollywood, Mrs. Leila Rogers testified in Washington that a movie called "None but the Lonely Heart" was un-American because it was "gloomy." This lady was the mother of a movie star named Ginger Rogers, and many did not think that she was peculiarly qualified to define, however negatively, the nature of American experience. But the fact is that this was one of those bungling insights like the one Mickey Rooney communicated when, dressed as Huck, he prayed to the Mississippi River. Mr. Rooney has been backed by T. S. Eliot, and Mrs. Rogers was also in excellent company.

The classic statement of her point of view was one made by William Dean Howells, who put it better, and also located the origin of the trouble in the place where the investigating committee expected to find it. "It is one of the reflections suggested by Dostoievsky's novel, *The Crime and the Punishment,*" Howells wrote, "that whoever struck a note so profoundly tragic in American fiction would do a false and mistaken thing. . . ." Here life is not so bad: "Our novelists, therefore, concern themselves with the more smiling aspects of life, which are the more American. . . ." It is "the large, cheerful average of health and success and happy life" which is "peculiarly American."

This opinion was later reinforced by Robert Frost in verse:

> It makes the guild of novel writers sick
> To be expected to be Dostoievskis
> On nothing worse than too much luck and comfort.

Just before this Frost had asked:

> How are we to write
> The Russian novel in America
> As long as life goes so unterribly?[1]

The Howells view of American experience is not the ignorant error it is often taken for. It is a half-truth or a partial truth⟦But there is an impressive body of evidence in our literature which presents the other part, contradicting cheer, health, success and happiness.⟧Commencing with our first Puritan writers, and coursing down through Poe, Hawthorne and Melville, say, and spreading widely in our own time, this literature often testifies for gloom indeed, and often for sickness, failure

[1] From "New Hampshire" from *Complete Poems of Robert Frost.* Copyright 1923 by Holt, Rinehart and Winston, Inc. Copyright 1951 by Robert Frost. Reprinted by permission of Holt, Rinehart and Winston, Inc.

and misery. And we have seen how even Mark Twain contributed in *Huckleberry Finn* bitterness, introversion, nightmare and death.

Hemingway was not alone, in contemporary literature, in presenting a picture of misery and sickness. It was long a common complaint against modern writing in general that it "refused to look on the good side." In a way there is sense in the observation, for although pessimism was by no means born with our century it is nevertheless an obvious feature of contemporary literature. This literature has many beginnings: in American fiction books like Crane's *Maggie* (1893) and Norris's *McTeague* (1899) stand out as landmarks. But often overlooked in our literary history is one particular moment at which something we recognize as more or less "modern" in our fiction—its frequent insistence on looking "only at the bad side"—may be said to have begun. This insistence, which writers of our time generally, and Hemingway specifically, have been charged with, had a kind of beginning one day in the mid-Nineties when Theodore Dreiser sat down and began "examining the current magazines." His dissatisfaction with what he found, recorded in *A Book About Myself* (1922), was epochal:

> I was never more confounded than by the discrepancy existing between my own observations and those displayed here, the beauty and peace and charm to be found in everything, the almost complete absence of any reference to the coarse and the vulgar and the cruel and the terrible. . . . Love was almost invariably rewarded . . . dreams came true . . . with such an air of assurance, omniscience and condescension, that I was quite put out by my own lacks and defects. They . . . wrote of nobility of character and sacrifice and the greatness of ideal and joy in simple things. . . . I had no such tales to tell, and, however much I tried, I could not think of any.

It happens that one of the writers Dreiser had been reading in the magazines was Howells himself. The disgust the younger man shows for a life in literature which he could not find elsewhere was a very large part of the motivation for his own work. It lasted him the better part of a writing lifetime, and it has survived him. Surrounded today by magazine fiction and movies, radio and television dramas, advertisements and the like, serious writers are driven to their insistence that cruelty and vulgarity exist, that love and dreams go sour. They are driven to it, as was Dreiser, because all about them is a world of "fiction" in the sense that it is "false." Part of their preoccupation with the darker sides of things comes from a completely human perversity that reacts in disgust from the piety and cant our people are fed commercially. For those who cannot accept the desperately censored pictures of life, with their fake satisfactions and sentimental sorrows, which "the current magazines" present, it is as though the statement of thesis brought with it the compulsion to antithesis. The serious writer who does nothing today to contradict or qualify "the greatness of ideals, and joy in simple things" becomes party to a conspiracy to ignore a good deal of what we all know to be real. Since the eighteenth century we have had a literature which reflects the health and happiness which American life affords, and it is quite proper that we should have too a literature which reflects and expresses the sickness and misery life in America also offers its people. And so we have novelists like Hemingway who help to right a balance which would otherwise weigh crazily on Howells' side.

Robert Frost—through no particular fault of his own the darling of the critics who most deplore Hemingway, and the recipient of four Pulitzer prizes and any number of honorary degrees—wrote of common sense, of wood smoke and apple orchards. Hemingway saw hysteria, and the smoke gunpowder makes, and knew the dull-green distillate of wormwood. Even through his melancholy—even in occasional desperation—Frost saw the eternal fields of New England, stitched together with stone walls, and in the distance the birches and the pine woods; Hemingway painted an American Guérnica. One takes sides in these matters, and thinks his opposition leaves out significant facts. But the argument as to which picture is American and which is not is misleading and premature. We do not know how things are going to come out, and to date both pictures reflect the nature of our experience, or neither does. We have had many years of peace and many wars. The face of America neither smiles with Howells or twitches with Hemingway. Or it does both, and even at once.

Hemingway's principal opposition has come from those who have attacked him for emphasizing the twitches, and for being pessimistic. Placing him in the flattering company of Joyce, Eliot and others, they complain passionately of his bitterness. Van Wyck Brooks, for example, demanded that modern writers have faith, faith in the goodness of human nature, for great literature has always had it, and had also health, will and courage. Hemingway, he protests, seems "bent on proving that life is a dark little pocket," and that "only the ugly is real." Brooks argues persuasively for the value of faith, but does not establish its basis. Other critics, too, have wanted Hemingway to write about "the good life."

These are familiar sounds, and even if *The Old Man and the*

Sea had not come along to mock them, rather hollow do they ring if one listens closely to the terms. The "goodness of human nature" is a phrase to give any man who reads his paper pause; "health" and "will" are words of barbed complexity for any thoughtful modern. As for "courage," it is the chief virtue in Hemingway's hierarchy of values, and certainly he tried very hard to show that many things beside the ugly—many women and many countries and their peoples—are real. It might be, though, that he would not have known exactly what is meant by "the good life" for never having lived enough of it.

No writer can write well about what he has not lived, known and found real for himself. One of the silliest minor spectacles our time affords with any regularity is that of critics telling writers what they should write about. It is hard to know precisely what the result of such counsel would be, because there are few clear-cut cases where anyone has paid much attention to such advice. But it would be a safe bet that capitulation would mean the end of any work that would outlast the moment. *Huckleberry Finn* is full of brutality and disgust, as well as of peace and content, because these are the things Clemens had known and felt and remembered. We should have forgot the book long ago, or never have read it, had this been otherwise. Hemingway's world is full of pain, and of moral, mental and physical wreck—and love and endurance and courage—because these are the things that were real to Ernest Hemingway. The critics make a mistake. You can tell a writer to go to hell, or stop reading him, or read him and tear him up, in private or in print. But you can't tell him what to write. If he is any good he writes what he knows and feels and that is the end of it as far as he is concerned.

It is a vague feeling of some critics, which is articulated by Brooks again, that the trouble with Hemingway came from his expatriation, which is the cardinal sin for nationalists. "When we leave our country," Brooks wrote in his *On Literature Today* (1941), "we are apt to leave our roots behind us, and we fail to develop roots in any other country." If anything at all has become clear by now it should be that if Hemingway had a hundred troubles this was not among them. Superficially, of course, his work did come to us by way of 27 rue de Fleurus, the Deux Magots, and the various hotels of Paris, Madrid, Havana and Venice where he labored. But at bottom the analysis is as mistaken as any single one could be, for although we can never know precisely what Hemingway learned abroad, we do know that he did not learn much of any great significance there that was not already available to him in the experience and traditions of his own country.

In its purely literary aspects, this is rather *like* the case of
Robert Frost, who is supposed to have learned in England how to
make poetry, instead of literary prose, out of the words and
rhythms of ordinary American speech. It might be true; maybe
Wilfred Gibson taught him all he knew. But Frost brought back
from England a "new" kind of writing which in its rural New
England diction is very like Thoreau, in its rural description very
like the best of Whittier and in its sentiments and speech rhythms
is like nothing so much as a well-known experimental poem of
Emerson's called "Hamatreya." We are in the process of develop-
ing our own literary traditions, or rather of discovering that we
have them. And while it would be suicidal to cut ourselves off from
the sources of things we require or can use, it does not hurt to
know what are the things we no longer have any need to import.[2]

It is even harder to know how Hemingway may be said to have
left his roots behind him when we were able to find the basic,
permeating pattern of his entire output with its source so deep in
one of the most native of all our books. The fact that for Huck and
for Nick the same experiences had identical results means among
other things that the smiling, sun-tanned mask which hides a pallor
that no smile brightens is an American mask for an American pallor. If Huck is truly American—and this has yet to be denied—then
so is the bitter, insomniacal, death-driven hero American, and
wholly so. Two of our most prominent heroes are casualties whom
the "knowledge of evil" we are commonly said to lack has made
sick. We are trying to get out of something when we attempt to
pin the blame for what we might not like in Hemingway on his
expatriation. It will not do, for he was aboriginal and the product
was home-grown.

America is a lucky country, and it is not surprising or unjust
that a great deal of our literature should reflect the smiling aspects
of our present and our past. But not every prospect pleases. To
keep a balance, and because many writers do not feel at all like
smiling, we get in the midst of healthy growth, death in the spring.
In the case of Hemingway we get it in a form and manner that are
made indigenous by his experience as a boy of life in this country
and by the clear and complete precedent of one of the greatest
and most compelling of all our native tales.

This theme of the boy shattered by the violence of the world
he grows up in is a variation on one of the most ancient of all
stories, and the greatest of all American stories, which relates the
meeting of innocence and experience. This was a theme of our first

[2] As result of this passage Frost was once asked what else, in his opinion, American writers had no need to import. He promptly answered "bourbon."

professional man of letters, Charles Brockden Brown, and in one way or another it seems now to have been at the very least the greatest theme of the second half of our nineteenth century. Here it was chiefly related at the very poles of our national experience —on the frontier and in Europe—as if tendencies are clearest when carried to their extremes. With a steady flow of travelers abroad at this time, it was primarily in Europe that the drama of the meeting of youth and age was enacted.

The story of the American in Europe had two rather separate developments. There was a crude, comic one, as the foremost humorists of the age—Artemus Ward, Mark Twain and Petroleum V. Nasby—each in turn wrote his account of innocents abroad. This version can be traced at home back to Seba Smith and the "stage Yankee" before it fades into its folk origins, where various rural native types confront city slickers or foreign aristocrats. But the theme was potentially rich in many other ways, as the European fiction of Nathaniel Hawthorne, William Dean Howells and Henry James shows. It is of course in James, on the European end, that the matter gets its fullest development. Inclined to simplify the two sides of the conflict himself (though of course less than this), James' picture of the American visitor under the impact of the European social order was a picture of simplicity, benevolence, naïveté and virtue struggling with complexity, sophistication, and even corruption and evil.

This story of innocence leaving its home and coming up against things which are not innocent is a great American story because it is based not only on the experience of every man as he grows up but also on the particular and peculiar historical experience of this nation. Once the country was fully discovered and established, we began after the Civil War to rediscover the world, and this adventure resulted in our defining ourselves in the light of people who did not seem, to us or to them, quite like us. In one way the definitions came back alike from both the frontier and the European poles, and the ways in which the definitions were changed by experience were similar. Huck's simplicity is complicated; *The American* Christopher Newman is a lot less naïve at the end than he was at the start; and by the end of "Daisy Miller" the girl is dead.

The Huck-Nick story shares this theme, for again it tells what happens when a spontaneous virtue meets with something that is not at all itself. But it is a variant, because there are differences here which change everything. Despite the fact that the traveling comedians made spectacles of their ignorance, they usually had the last laugh. And though in their contact with Europe the more serious pilgrims were usually enriched at their pain, more often than not they had showed up well in the process, by virtue of a kind of power that comes from purity. But there is nothing subtle about the force that confronts the natural goodness of Huck and Nick. It is violence, which is an essential experience of the frontier and also—in our time, which is a war time—of the American in Europe. And this time there is nothing in any way triumphant about the beating which innocence takes, or about what happens to it after it is beaten.

The repetition of Twain's story by Hemingway establishes a continuity of American experience from one century to another, and vastly reinforces the meaning of either story taken separately. When across the generations we take twice to ourselves the same pattern we should know that it has more to say to us than we heard at first. When a story is repeated it is sanctified by tradition. It proves too that it has a vitality that may not have been immediately evident, and a significance that is not apparent on the surface. And when the tale also explains something, in an imaginary and narrative way, we call it a "myth."

Myths are stories which have something about them that we clumsily call "magic." They have a special quality, an aura of portent. They deal, normally, with some critical phase of life, some crisis. The figures who undergo the adventures of the tale take on a symbolic air because we begin to recognize some aspect of our own. In an imaginative way we participate in myths, and the more we are able to do this, the more meaning they have for us. Of course we know that myths are false, as matters of fact. But they can be so profound as matters of metaphor that they make the facts seem superficial, and even accidental.

The story of the adventures of Huck Finn and the Hemingway hero is such a myth, which relates once more the Fall of Man, the loss of Paradise. But it is a myth for Americans, which speaks to the people of the country from whose experience it springs, saying: We start out smiling, and well disposed toward the world and our fellows. We are made in the image of this naturally good, simple, innocent boy, eager and expectant. But in the process of our going out, and when we meet with life, we are struck down, and afterward nothing in the kingdom can put us all the way back together again.

The boy was bright-eyed at first. But then, soon, on one side of him were the twisting inhibitions and distortions of domestic life, and on the other a brutality and pain he had no reason under heaven to expect in a world of men who should be as goodhearted as he. In a tight and tortured place, he lights out in rebellion from the life of the world his elders have made and thrust on him. And then it is that he is really smashed, for the small world opens on a greater one that is much worse. His adventures there disqualify him from ever returning to the life he has deserted, and the world he has run away to becomes more and more a land of horror until finally he is hit hard and for good. Broken now, and pale and sick at heart, he rebels wholly. He can never be completely reconciled, and he has a permanent need for defense and escape.

The epic, national hero, call him Huck or Hemingway's, is virile and all-outdoors, but he is sick. He is told that as an American he does not "think," he has no "mind." But after what he has been through, mind and thought mean misery; his simplicity is forced on him and he dares not let it go.

This myth says something about us that is rather wistful. But it is as eloquent as any voice we can speak with of an innocent desire for a decent life on the one hand, and a sense of terrible betrayal on the other. We would do justly and be kind, it says. We wished no evil. But as we grew up it was everywhere, and all our expectations were sold out. This is as deep, and as great and beautiful, as any myth we have. It tries to explain us to ourselves and to a world that does not comprehend—and understandably does not, since it sees not our morning wishes but the mess that has been made of them by afternoon. It also tries to explain why it is that despite all our other, opposing myths—of success, progress, the certain beneficence of technical advance and the like—we are neither happy nor whole, nor, for the most part, kind and completely decent ourselves. It says with overwhelming poignance: We *would* have been, we *could* have been, but we were crippled before we were grown by the world we were given to grow in and now it is too late.

It was a lovely world for Huck and Nick, with its rivers and woods and at first unspoiled. But the natural beauty of the land was a part of the betrayal, by which they were lulled into letting down defenses and misled into expecting only the best. The original beauty of the country and a breathless anticipation of the possibilities of life here in what seemed the newest and most promising world since Eden were part of a seduction that went bad and should have ended at the doctor's.

Thus we try to explain our experience. We believed all the visions were true and went abroad. But they were false. Someone stuck his head out and smiled and it was smashed. He asked only that others be as honest and as well disposed as he, but they were not and the damage is done and for good. It was treason, and the response must be extreme. It is. Finally there is only one defense left. It is an escape which is the same escape either way, down or across the river. It is a flight from violence and evil which Mark Twain once dreamed, and which Hemingway's life and Hemingway's work eternally rehearsed.

Selected Bibliography

PRIMARY SOURCES

Only the major published works are listed here. For additional items—both published and unpublished—see the entries below for Audre Hanneman and for Philip Young and Charles W. Mann under the heading "Secondary Sources: Bibliographical Materials."

Three Stories and Ten Poems. Paris and Dijon: Contact Publishing Company, 1923.

in our time. Paris: Three Mountains Press, 1924.

In Our Time. New York: Boni and Liveright, 1925.

The Torrents of Spring. New York: Scribner's, 1926.

The Sun Also Rises. New York: Scribner's, 1926.

Men Without Women. New York: Scribner's, 1927.

A Farewell to Arms. New York: Scribner's, 1929.

Death in the Afternoon. New York: Scribner's, 1932.

Winner Take Nothing. New York: Scribner's, 1933.

Green Hills of Africa. New York: Scribner's, 1935.

To Have and Have Not. New York: Scribner's, 1937.

The Fifth Column and the First Forty-nine Stories. New York: Scribner's, 1938.

For Whom the Bell Tolls. New York: Scribner's, 1940.

Across the River and Into the Trees. New York: Scribner's, 1950.

The Old Man and the Sea. New York: Scribner's, 1952.

Books Published Posthumously
Fiction

The Fifth Column and Four Stories of the Spanish Civil War. New York: Scribner's, 1969.

Islands in the Stream. New York: Scribner's, 1970.

Nonfiction

The Wild Years. Ed. Gene Z. Hanrahan. New York: Dell, 1962. A
     collection of seventy-three articles Hemingway wrote for the
     Toronto Star.
A Moveable Feast. New York: Scribner's, 1964.
*By-Line: Ernest Hemingway (Selected Articles and Dispatches of
     Four Decades).* Ed. William White. New York: Scribner's,
     1967.
Ernest Hemingway, Cub Reporter: Kansas City Star Stories. Ed.
     M. Bruccoli, Pittsburgh: University of Pittsburgh Press, 1970.
Ernest Hemingway's Apprenticeship: Oak Park, 1916–1917. Ed. M.
     Bruccoli. Washington, D.C.: NCR Microcard Editions, 1971.
     Early writings for the Oak Park High School *Tabula* and
     Trapeze.

SECONDARY SOURCES

Bibliographical Materials

Beebe, Maurice, and John Feaster. "Criticism of Ernest Heming-
     way: A Selected Checklist." *Modern Fiction Studies,* 14, no. 3
     (Autumn 1968), 337–69.
Hanneman, Audre. *Ernest Hemingway: A Comprehensive Bibliog-
     raphy.* Princeton: Princeton University Press, 1967.
————. "Hanneman Addenda." In *Fitzgerald/Hemingway Annual,
     1970,* pp. 195–218. Washington, D.C.: NCR Microcard Edi-
     tions, 1970.
Young, Philip, and Charles W. Mann. *The Hemingway Manu-
     scripts: An Inventory.* University Park: Pennsylvania State
     University Press, 1969.

Biography

Baker, Carlos. *Ernest Hemingway: A Life Story.* New York: Scrib-
     ner's, 1969.
Callaghan, Morley. *That Summer in Paris.* New York: Coward-
     McCann, 1963.
Cowley, Malcolm. "A Portrait of Mr. Papa." *Life,* Jan. 10, 1949, pp.
     86–101.
Hemingway, Leicester. *My Brother, Ernest Hemingway.* Cleve-
     land: World, 1962.
Hotchner, A. E. *Papa Hemingway.* New York: Random House,
     1966.
Loeb, Harold. *The Way It Was.* New York: Criterion, 1959.

Montgomery, Constance Cappel. *Hemingway in Michigan.* New York: Fleet, 1966.

Ross, Lillian. *Portrait of Hemingway.* New York: Simon and Schuster, 1961.

Sanford, Marcelline Hemingway. *At the Hemingways: A Family Portrait.* Boston: Atlantic, Little-Brown, 1962.

Stein, Gertrude. *The Autobiography of Alice B. Toklas.* New York: Literary Guild, 1933.

Criticism

Books

Atkins, John. *The Art of Ernest Hemingway: His Work and Personality.* Rev. ed. London: Spring Books, n.d. First published London: P. Nevill, 1952.

Baker, Carlos. *Hemingway: The Writer as Artist.* Princeton: Princeton University Press, 1952, 1956; 3rd, enlarged ed., 1963.

Baker, Sheridan. *Ernest Hemingway.* New York: Holt, Rinehart, 1967.

Benson, Jackson J. *Hemingway: The Writer's Art of Self-Defense.* Minneapolis: University of Minnesota Press, 1969.

DeFalco, Joseph. *The Hero in Hemingway's Short Stories.* Pittsburgh: University of Pittsburgh Press, 1963.

Fenton, Charles A. *The Apprenticeship of Ernest Hemingway: The Early Years.* New York: Farrar, Straus, 1954; rpt. Compass Books, 1958.

Hovey, Richard B. *Hemingway: The Inward Terrain.* Seattle: University of Washington Press, 1969.

Joost, Nicholas. *Ernest Hemingway and the Little Magazines: The Paris Years.* Barre, Mass.: Barre Publishers, 1968.

Killinger, John. *Hemingway and the Dead Gods: A Study in Existentialism.* Lexington: University of Kentucky Press, 1960.

Lewis, Robert W., Jr. *Hemingway on Love.* Austin: University of Texas Press, 1965.

Peterson, Richard K. *Hemingway, Direct and Oblique.* The Hague: Mouton, 1969.

Rovit, Earl. *Ernest Hemingway.* New York: Twayne, 1963.

Sanderson, Stewart. *Hemingway.* Edinburgh: Oliver and Boyd, 1961.

Stephens, Robert O. *Hemingway's Non-Fiction: The Public Voice.* Chapel Hill: University of North Carolina Press, 1968.

Waldhorn, Arthur. *A Reader's Guide to Ernest Hemingway.* New York: Farrar, Straus, and Giroux, 1972.

Watts, Emily. *Ernest Hemingway and the Arts.* Urbana: University of Illinois Press, 1971.

Wylder, Delbert E. *Hemingway's Heroes.* Albuquerque: University of New Mexico Press, 1970.

Young, Philip. *Ernest Hemingway.* New York: Rinehart, 1952 [Enlarged with an introduction and afterword as *Ernest Hemingway: A Reconsideration.* New York: Harcourt, Brace, 1966.].

Anthologies

Asselineau, Roger, ed. *The Literary Reputation of Hemingway in Europe.* Paris: Minard, 1965; New York: New York University Press, 1965.

Baker, Carlos, ed. *Critiques of Four Major Novels.* Scribner Research Anthologies. New York: Scribner's, 1962.

———. *Hemingway and His Critics: An International Anthology.* New York: Hill and Wang, 1961.

Bruccoli, Matthew, and C. E. Frazer Clark, Jr., eds. *Fitzgerald/Hemingway Annual.* Washington, D.C.: NCR Microcard Editions, 1969– .

McCaffery, John K. M., ed. *Ernest Hemingway: The Man and His Work.* Cleveland: World, 1950.

Modern Fiction Studies. Ernest Hemingway: Special Number, 14, no. 3 (Autumn 1968).

Weeks, Robert P., ed. *Hemingway: A Collection of Critical Essays.* Englewood Cliffs, N.J.: Prentice-Hall, 1962.

General Essays

Aldridge, John W. *After the Lost Generation,* pp. 23–43. New York: Noonday, 1958.

Backman, Melvin. "Hemingway: The Matador and the Crucified." *Modern Fiction Studies,* 1 (August 1955), 2–11. [Reprinted in Baker, *Hemingway and His Critics,* pp. 245–58; and in Baker, *Critiques of Four Major Novels,* pp. 135–43.]

Beach, Joseph Warren. "Ernest Hemingway: The Esthetics of Simplicity." In *American Fiction: 1920–1940,* pp. 97–119. New York: Macmillan, 1941.

Bishop, John Peale. "The Missing All." *Virginia Quarterly Review,* 13 (Summer 1937), 107–21. [Reprinted in McCaffery, *Ernest Hemingway: The Man and His Work,* pp. 292–307.]

Bridgman, Richard. "Ernest Hemingway." In *The Colloquial Style in America,* pp. 195–230. New York: Oxford University Press, 1966.

Brooks, Cleanth. "Ernest Hemingway: Man on His Moral Uppers." In *The Hidden God,* pp. 6–21. New Haven: Yale University Press, 1963.

Burgum, Edwin B. "Ernest Hemingway and the Psychology of the Lost Generation," In *The Novel and the World's Dilemma,* pp. 184–204. New York: Oxford University Press, 1947.

Cargill, Oscar. *Intellectual America: Ideas on the March,* pp. 351–70. New York: Macmillan, 1941.

Carpenter, Frederic I. "Hemingway Achieves the Fifth Dimension." *PMLA,* 69 (September 1954), 711–18. [Reprinted in Frederic I. Carpenter, *American Literature and the Dream,* pp. 185–93 (New York: Philosophical Library, 1954); and in Baker, *Hemingway and His Critics,* pp. 192–201.]

Colvert, James B. "Ernest Hemingway's Morality in Action." *American Literature,* 27 (November 1955), 372–85.

Cowley, Malcolm. "Nightmare and Ritual in Hemingway." Introduction to *The Viking Portable Hemingway.* New York, Viking, 1944. [Reprinted in Weeks, *Hemingway: A Collection of Critical Essays,* pp. 40–51.]

———. "A Portrait of Mr. Papa." *Life,* January 10, 1949, pp. 86–101. [Reprinted in McCaffery, *Ernest Hemingway: The Man and His Work,* pp. 34–56.]

Eastman, Max. "Bull in the Afternoon." *New Republic,* June 7, 1933, pp. 94–97. [Reprinted in McCaffery, *Ernest Hemingway: The Man and His Work,* pp. 66–75.]

Fiedler, Leslie. *Love and Death in the American Novel,* pp. 304–9, 350–52. New York: Criterion, 1960.

Fuchs, Daniel. "Ernest Hemingway, Literary Critic." *American Literature,* 36 (1965), 431-51.

Graham, John. "Ernest Hemingway: The Meaning of Style." *Modern Fiction Studies,* 6 (Winter 1960–61), 298–313.

Halliday, E. M. "Hemingway's Ambiguity: Symbolism and Irony." *American Literature,* 28 (March 1956), 1–22. [Reprinted in Baker, *Critiques of Four Major Novels,* pp. 174–82; and in Weeks, *Hemingway: A Collection of Critical Essays,* pp. 52–71.]

Kashkeen, Ivan. "Ernest Hemingway: A Tragedy of Craftsmanship." *International Literature,* 5 (1935). [Reprinted in McCaffery, *Ernest Hemingway: The Man and His Work,* pp. 76–108.]

Levin, Harry. "Observations on the Style of Ernest Hemingway." *Kenyon Review,* 13 (Autumn 1951), 581–609. [Reprinted in Harry Levin, *Contexts of Criticism* (Cambridge: Harvard University Press, 1957); in Baker, *Hemingway and His Critics,* pp. 93-115; and in Weeks, *Hemingway: A Collection of Critical Essays,* pp. 72-85.]

Lewis, Wyndham. "Ernest Hemingway: The 'Dumb Ox.'" In *Men Without Art,* pp. 17-40. London: Cassell, 1934.

O'Faolain, Sean. *The Vanishing Hero: Studies in Novelists of the Twentieth Century,* pp. 112-45. Boston: Little, Brown, 1956.

Oldsey, Bern. "The Snows of Ernest Hemingway." *Wisconsin Studies in Contemporary Literature,* 4 (Spring-Summer 1963), 172-98.

Paolini, Pier Francesco. "The Hemingway of the Major Works." *Letterature Moderne* 6 (November-December, 1956). [Reprinted in Baker, *Hemingway and His Critics,* pp. 131-44.]

Plimpton, George. "The Art of Fiction XXI." *Paris Review,* 18 (Spring 1958), 60-89. [Reprinted in *Writers at Work: The "Paris Review" Interviews,* pp. 215-39, second series (New York: Viking, 1963); and in Baker, *Hemingway and His Critics,* pp. 19-37.]

Savage, D. S. "Ernest Hemingway." In *The Withered Branch: Six Studies in the Modern Novel,* pp. 23-43. London: Eyre and Spottiswoode, 1950.

Schwartz, Delmore. "Ernest Hemingway's Literary Situation." *Southern Review,* 3 (1938), 769-82. [Reprinted in McCaffery, *Ernest Hemingway: The Man and His Work,* pp. 114-29.]

Tanner, Tony. "Ernest Hemingway's Unhurried Sensations." In *The Reign of Wonder: Naivity and Reality in American Literature,* pp. 228-57. Cambridge: Cambridge University Press, 1965.

Trilling, Lionel. "Hemingway and His Critics." *Partisan Review,* 6 (Winter 1939), 52-60. [Reprinted in Baker, *Hemingway and His Critics,* pp. 61-70.]

Warren, Robert Penn. "Ernest Hemingway." *Kenyon Review,* 9 (Winter 1947), 1-28. [Reprinted as Introduction to Modern Standard Authors edition of *A Farewell to Arms* (New York: Scribner's, 1949); in J. W. Aldridge, ed., *Critiques and Essays on Modern Fiction,* pp. 447-73 (New York: Ronald, 1952); and in M. D. Zabel, ed., *Literary Opinion in America* pp. 447-60 (New York: Harper, 1951).]

West, Ray B. "The Failure of Sensibility." *Sewanee Review,* 53 (Winter 1945), 120-35. [Reprinted in Walton Litz, ed., *Modern American Fiction,* pp. 244-255 (New York: Oxford University Press, 1963).]

Wilson, Edmund. "Hemingway: Bourdon Gauge of Morale." In

The Wound and the Bow, pp. 214–42. Boston: Houghton, Mifflin, 1941. [Reprinted in McCaffery, *Ernest Hemingway: The Man and His Work,* pp. 236–57.]

————. *The Shores of Light: A Literary Chronicle of the 20's and 30's,* pp. 115–24, 339–44, 616–29. New York: Farrar, Straus, 1952.

Essays on the novels (Note: This list is rigorously selective. The reader should consult also the essays about these novels in the *books* cited above. The order of novels given below is chronological, based on dates of publication.)

The Sun Also Rises

Adams, R. P. "Sunrise out of the Waste Land." *Tulane Studies in English,* 9 (1959), 119–31.

Farrell, James T. "The Sun Also Rises." In *The League of Frightened Philistines.* New York: Vanguard, 1945. [Reprinted in Baker, *Critiques of Four Major Novels,* pp. 4–6; and in McCaffery, *Ernest Hemingway: The Man and His Work,* pp. 221–25.]

Scott, Arthur L. "In Defense of Robert Cohn." *College English,* 18 (March 1957), 309–14.

Spilka, Mark. "The Death of Love in *The Sun Also Rises.*" In *Twelve Original Essays on Great American Novels,* edited by Charles Shapiro, pp. 238–56. Detroit: Wayne State University Press, 1958. [Reprinted in Baker, *Hemingway and His Critics,* pp. 80–92; and in Weeks, *Hemingway: A Collection of Critical Essays,* pp. 127–38.]

Woolf, Virginia. "An Essay in Criticism." In *Granite and Rainbow,* pp. 85–92. London: Hogarth, 1958.

A Farewell to Arms

Anderson, Charles R. "Hemingway's Other Style." *Modern Language Notes,* 76 (May 1961), 434–42. [Reprinted in Baker, *Critiques of Four Major Novels,* pp. 41–46.]

Ford, Ford Madox. Introduction *A Farewell to Arms* by Ernest Hemingway. New York: Modern Library, 1932.

Gerstenberger, Donna. "The Waste Land in *A Farewell to Arms,*" *Modern Language Notes,* 66 (1961), 24–25.

Hemingway, Ernest. "The Original Conclusion to *A Farewell to Arms.*" In Baker, *Critiques of Four Major Novels,* p. 75.

West, Ray B., Jr. "A Farewell to Arms." In Ray B. West, Jr., and R. W. Stallman, *The Art of Modern Fiction,* pp. 662–33. New York: Rinehart, 1949. [Reprinted in Baker, *Critiques of Four*

Major Novels, pp. 28–36; and in Weeks, *Hemingway: A Collection of Critical Essays,* pp. 139–51.]

To Have and Have Not

Cowley, Malcolm. "Hemingway: Work in Progress." In *Think Back on Us: A Contemporary Chronicle of the 1930's,* edited by H. D. Piper, pp. 310–14. Carbondale: Southern Illinois University Press, 1967.

Grebstein, S. N. "The Tough Hemingway and His Hard-Boiled Children." In *Tough Guy Writers of the Thirties,* edited by David Madden, pp. 18–41. Carbondale: Southern Illinois University Press, 1968.

Young, Philip. "Focus on *To Have and Have Not.*" In *Tough Guy Writers of the Thirties,* edited by David Madden, pp. 42–50. Carbondale: Southern Illinois University Press, 1968.

For Whom the Bell Tolls

Barea, Arturo. "Not Spain but Hemingway." *Horizon,* 3 (May 1941), 350–61. [Reprinted in Baker, *Hemingway and His Critics,* pp. 202–12.]

Fenimore, Edward. "English and Spanish in *For Whom the Bell Tolls.*" *ELH,* 10 (1943), 73–86. [Reprinted in McCaffery, *Ernest Hemingway: The Man and His Work,* pp. 205–20.]

MacDonald, Dwight. "Reading from Left to Right." *Partisan Review,* 8 (January–February 1941), 24–28.

Schorer, Mark. "The Background of a Style." *Kenyon Review,* 3 (Winter 1941), 101–5. [Reprinted in Baker, *Critiques of Four Major Novels,* pp. 87–89.]

Trilling, Lionel. "An American in Spain." In *The Partisan Reader,* edited by W. Phillips and P. Rahv, pp. 639–44. New York: Dial, 1946.

Across the River and Into the Trees

Lisca, Peter. "The Structure of Hemingway's *Across the River and Into the Trees.*" *Modern Fiction Studies,* 12 (Summer 1966), 232–50.

Oppel, Horst. "Hemingway's *Across the River and Into the Trees.*" In Baker, *Hemingway and His Critics,* pp. 213–26.

Rosenfeld, Isaac. "A Farewell to Hemingway." *Kenyon Review,* 13 (Winter 1951), 147–55.

The Old Man and the Sea

Burhans, Clinton S., Jr. "*The Old Man and the Sea:* Hemingway's Tragic Vision of Man." *American Literature,* 31 (January